GUIDED NUMEROLOGY WORKBOOK

GUIDED NUMEROLOGY WORKBOOK

A Beginner's Guide to Understanding Yourself through Your Numbers

KELLI MILLER

Foreword by Stefanie Caponi

Illustrated by Coni Curi

Zeitgeist • New York

For Paige, Haley, Christian, and Steven, my
eternal stars, always illuminating my journey with
unconditional love, joy, and gratitude

Published in the United States by Zeitgeist™, an imprint and
division of Penguin Random House LLC, New York.
zeitgeistpublishing.com

Zeitgeist™ is a trademark of Penguin Random House LLC.
ISBN: 9780593886373

Illustrations by Coni Curi
Book design by Emma Hall
Author photograph © by Caitlin Manley
Illustrator photograph © 2020 by Ignacio Sanchez
Edited by Sarah Curley

Printed in the United States of America
1st Printing

Contents

Foreword 7

Introduction 9

Glossary 14

Chapter 1

EXPLORING THE NUMBERS 17

Chapter 2

UNCOVERING YOUR CORE NUMBERS 57

Chapter 3

EXPLORING YOUR CYCLES 113

Chapter 4

DECODING YOUR CHARTS 163

Chapter 5

SHARING THE ART OF NUMEROLOGY 195

Conclusion 207

Resources 209

Index 210

Acknowledgments 219

FOREWORD

During my 33rd year I experienced my first spiritual awakening. I found myself moving away from the parts of my life that had provided stability: my job, my marriage, and the activities that once brought me joy. As I embraced this awakening, I sought answers to why my life was falling apart. I began to notice repeating numbers all around me, specifically 33 and 333. These numbers were everywhere: clocks, microwaves, license plates—even billboards. A quick internet search opened my eyes to the world of numerology and the hidden meanings behind the numbers that were following me around. I was no stranger to the numerological significance of the major and minor arcana cards of the tarot and their relationship to the signs and planets in astrology, but numerology added a brand-new layer of connection to the magic and mystery of the universe. Suddenly I didn't feel so alone.

Author and psychic medium Kelli Miller has been assisting spiritual seekers for over a decade after the pull from the spirit became too strong to ignore. Like myself, she was called to learn more about the messages encoded in each numerical sign the universe dropped along her path. *Guided Numerology Workbook* contains in-depth explanations of the sacred energy contained within each number and how they can become beacons of light and truth. The inclusion of the tarot and astrological correlations adds to the importance of incorporating numerology into your spiritual arsenal.

Within the pages of *Guided Numerology Workbook*, Miller breaks down the language of numbers along with how your name and birthday are your cosmic blueprint for understanding yourself, your purpose, areas for growth, and so much more in a fun, approachable, and practical way. Miller has put together a comprehensive, step-by-step workbook that will assist you in calculating your unique numerology in several life-changing categories, including your Life Path Number, your Inner Soul Number, and even how numerology plays a significant role in the year, month, and day you are having. Understanding your Core Numbers and the way numerology affects each season of life will guide you to greater self-understanding and acceptance.

Knowing your numerology is not only empowering for your personal journey (I learned that I have multiple connections to Master Number 11, which is associated with a strong intuition and helping guide others along their spiritual paths—a lovely surprise synchronicity I have in common with the author, who I believe is the perfect person to share the exciting world of numerology with you!). You will also be able to calculate the numerology of your loved ones, an invaluable tool for relational healing and strengthening existing bonds. Using this book to calculate my spouse's, parents', siblings', and my own child's numerology has led me to a new understanding of our unique relationships within this lifetime.

The universe is always communicating with you, offering support and guidance. The activities within *Guided Numerology Workbook* will direct your path to speaking the numerological language of the universe, forever changing your perception of seemingly casual glances at the clock and seeing the number 2:22 or noticing your house numbers reduce down to the number 6. Now you will be able to interpret numbers with confidence, harnessing their power to help you embrace your own unique numerological energy and embody your most authentic self.

Stefanie Caponi

INTRODUCTION

When I began my deep spiritual journey in 2011, I was so confused by the transformation I was experiencing. So much was happening at once, and I had no idea what much of it meant! My reaction was to read all I could on metaphysics and spirituality in an attempt to gain some clarity. When I stumbled upon numerology and discovered my Life Path Number, 11, everything clicked into place. I understood the causes of my innate psychic abilities, why people are drawn to me, and the source of my deeply contemplative nature. This one field of study connected everything, from crystals to frequencies. During that time of exploration, numerology led to significant, tremendous revelations that touched my spirit deeply, and it became the key to unlocking many of the questions I've always had about myself.

One of my hopes in writing this book is that it may do the same for you.

A core tenet of numerology is that each of us is more than a single number; rather, we are all complex individuals with unique personalities and unending potential. That's why the primary tool for self-understanding in numerology is the numerology chart, a customized group of numbers derived from your unique information, including your name and birth date. Your numerology chart encompasses many numbers, each of which helps illustrate the depths of your identity, sometimes illuminating facets of yourself that you had yet to discover. (We'll walk through calculating your own chart in this workbook.)

Numerology is an ancient practice that assigns specific meanings to numbers and—based on those meanings and a few simple calculations—helps people decode messages about their personalities and destinies. It interprets the energy vibrations that numbers contain to offer symbolic significance to its students. Among the many ancient traditions that have gained recent popularity, numerology has seen a rebirth because it can lead so directly to increased awareness of spirituality and personal development. It's a practice that people are using to better understand themselves and deal with life's challenges, as well as a popular technique for sound advice and self-discovery.

Although numerology revolves around multiple numbers that are significant to you as an individual, many experts believe that the most important among them is your Life Path Number. This single number—calculated using your full birth date—describes your possible life purpose on Earth. Multiple esoteric schools of thought say that your unique character's deeply ingrained natural attributes, traits, and inclinations are symbolized by your birth date, so it makes sense that your Life Path Number would be calculated using those specific digits. The challenges and lessons you'll encounter over your lifetime are also described by your Life Path Number. It's the star of the show!

But the other numbers in your chart round it out, painting a rich and full portrait of who you truly are. Along with your Life Path Number, your Birth Day, First Impression, Inner Soul, Character, and Expression Numbers create a set called your Core Numbers. Dig a little deeper and you'll unlock your Character Number, which highlights your core qualities and values. Your Cycle and Karmic Numbers provide insights into the karmic teachings and cyclical patterns that impact your life. And when all of these figures are examined together, they provide a robust picture of your distinct personality.

The incorporation of gemstone connections, astrology, and tarot with numerology provides a multifaceted approach to self-understanding and enhances the interpretive framework. These complementary divination methods—each with their own history and approach—connect meaningfully with numerology to offer supplementary insights. They overlap in their goal of providing insights into your personality, life purpose, and spiritual path. I've included many of those connections throughout this workbook so you can explore and experiment with them.

But, naturally, our main focus will be on calculating the numbers in your chart and understanding what they say about you as a person. Learning about numerology and beginning to uncover the mysteries contained in your chart is an exciting way to kick-start your journey of self-discovery and self-development. As you learn how these numbers work and what their energies and meanings represent, you'll dive deeper into understanding yourself as a unique individual.

In addition to revealing your essential self, understanding your numerological chart helps you recognize your skills and abilities, empowering you to realize your full potential. It also sheds light on opportunities for personal development and self-improvement, helping you accept your most authentic self and come to terms with your shortcomings. Basically, your chart is a valuable tool for deep internal examination. It contains energy that, when understood and aligned with your most authentic self, may help you build more harmony, fulfillment, and purpose in all aspects of your life.

Sounds pretty amazing, right? But just where did all of this digit-centric wisdom come from in the first place?

A BRIEF HISTORY OF NUMEROLOGY

Greek philosopher and mathematician Pythagoras is credited with laying the foundation for the most widely practiced modern numerological system about 2,000 years ago. Pythagoras believed that mathematical principles might be used to understand the universe, so he created a system in which every number from one to nine was assigned a distinct energy and symbolism, giving certain numbers particular meanings.

Even before Pythagoras created the system we use today, many ancient cultures—including the Babylonians, Greeks, and Egyptians—used other forms of numerology to guide their lives. They made judgments about religion, architecture, and even governance using mathematics as well as consulting numbers to understand the natural world and forecast future events. Numerology had an impact on everything back then, from religious rituals to everyday worries.

And although Pythagorean numerology eventually became the dominant style—especially in Western cultures—several other numerological systems are still practiced globally. Kabbalah numerology is a Jewish esoteric teaching system that explores the spiritual significance of numbers; Chinese numerology assigns meanings to numbers based on their association with the five elements and the cosmic energies influencing people's lives; and Chaldean numerology calculates the outer personality based on a single digit and the inner personality based on two digits. Each numerological system provides distinct views and viewpoints, giving practitioners access to diverse instruments for self-exploration, guidance, and understanding the world around them.

Some practitioners specialize in these non-Pythagorean systems, but the style of numerology we'll explore in this book originated with Pythagoras's theories. His is still among the most prominent applications of numerology in use today. Pythagorean numerology's ease of use, intellectual depth, and cultural integration contributed to its quick rise in popularity. By assigning each alphabetic letter a numeric value, modern numerology can analyze both names and birth dates to provide insights into future outcomes, life pathways, and personality traits. It's fairly simple and easy to learn, but it also gives you a staggering depth of insight and self-understanding.

NUMEROLOGY AS A WINDOW TO THE SELF

Numerology is all about you as an individual. Working with the key numbers in your chart will help you see your most fundamental qualities, your life path, and your potential more clearly than ever before. With step-by-step instructions, this book acts as a guide to help you calculate and create your numerology chart.

You'll need your full birth name to start this trip because it contains the vibrational essence of who you are. Your full birth date is also necessary to identify significant numerological influences. And the final piece of the puzzle? Your open mind, which will lead you to new discoveries and insights.

Because Core Numbers and numerological cycles are fundamental to comprehending and interpreting your entire chart, this book starts by introducing them. As you go through the steps of working with your Core Numbers, more details will reveal themselves to you, progressively creating a complete picture of your unique and personal numerological profile.

This book's chapters, activities, and reflections will assist you in developing a stronger relationship with numerology and incorporating your newfound understanding of yourself. Although certain calculations may seem difficult at first, this book offers clear instructions and plenty of help to get you through the exercises with ease.

As you work your way through this book, you'll learn about reading for other people as well as for yourself, but I've made sure to point out the ethical issues of doing so. Getting permission before reading for someone else is a must, and when conducting a numerology reading for someone else, it's important to be mindful of not revealing too much personal information about them to others, thereby ensuring that their privacy is respected. You are encouraged to enter this book with a healthy respect for your own boundaries and the boundaries of others. This will help to promote a responsible and compassionate attitude to practicing numerology.

CHOSEN NAMES AND BIRTH DATES IN NUMEROLOGY

The simplest and most widely used methods for calculating your Core Numbers use your full birth date and the full name assigned to you at birth—all the stuff that's printed on your original birth certificate.

But that doesn't work for us all. Some of us have gone through marriages, divorces, or gender-affirming surgeries. Some of us have changed our names to protect ourselves. Some of us use stage names or pen names that become crucial and permanent parts of our identities. These changes affect us deeply.

If you have a different chosen name that resonates for you more deeply than the one assigned to you at birth, use that name in your numerological chart calculations. If the day you legally or officially made that name change felt like a rebirth, use that date as your chosen birth day.

By definition, your chosen name will carry a different frequency than your birth name, and so will your chosen birth day. If you're curious, you can run your chart using both names and both dates and see how they compare. Which one more accurately reflects the person you are today?

GLOSSARY

A glossary is usually found at the back of a book, but because numerology includes so many specific and similar-sounding terms, this glossary appears right up front. We'll explore all of these ideas in depth in the coming chapters, but here's a little preview . . . and a cheat sheet to peek at if you forget the difference between your Expression Number and your First Impression Number.

ARCHETYPE: Every number in numerology symbolizes a character type with distinct characteristics, life lessons, and vibrations, all impacting personality, conduct, and life path.

ARROWS: Specific patterns formed by the arrangement of numbers in a numerology chart. They provide insights into key strengths, challenges, and potential paths of growth for a person.

BIRTH DAY NUMBER: A core element of an individual's numerology chart, derived from their birth date. It offers insights into the individual's personality traits, strengths, and potential challenges.

BIRTH PATH CHART: A numerological chart that maps out the numeric influences present at the time of an individual's birth. It includes the Birth Day Number, Day Number, and other relevant numbers derived from the birth date.

CHARACTER NUMBER: A number calculated using the consonants in an individual's full birth name. It represents the outward expression of their personality and impacts how they present themselves to the world.

CONCORDS: In numerology, harmonious relationships between numbers in a numerology chart. They indicate areas of compatibility and alignment between different aspects of an individual's numerological profile.

CORE NUMBERS: An individual's Life Path Number, Birth Day Number, First Impression Number, Inner Soul Number, Character Number, and Expression Number.

DESTINY NUMBER: Also known as the Expression Number; a number calculated using the full birth name and reveals the individual's innate talents, abilities, and potential life path.

DIVINATION: In numerology, the use of the vibrational energy of numbers to analyze patterns and trends that provide direction and forecasts to predict someone's life, character, and future.

EXPRESSION NUMBER: Also known as the Destiny Number; a number calculated using the full birth name and reveals the individual's innate talents, abilities, and potential life path.

FIRST IMPRESSION NUMBER: A number derived from the consonants in an individual's full birth name. It represents the initial impression they make on others and influences their communication style and social interactions.

INCARNATION: A soul taking on a physical form during its journey through several lives. The vibrational energy of specific numbers can assist in the discovery of the spiritual causes for one's current situation in life as well as the soul's progress.

INNER SOUL NUMBER: Also known as the Soul Urge Number; a number calculated using the vowels in an individual's full birth name. It reveals their deepest desires, motivations, and spiritual aspirations.

KARMIC: Unfinished business, obstacles, or patterns carried over from previous incarnations. One must overcome these lessons to balance their karma and move forward on their soul's journey of spiritual development.

KARMIC DEBT NUMBER: A challenging aspect of an individual's numerology chart that highlights unresolved karmic lessons from past lives. It represents areas of personal growth and transformation that require attention and resolution in this lifetime.

KARMIC LESSON NUMBER: A number calculated using the full birth name and reveals the karmic influences affecting the individual's expression and communication style.

LIFE PATH NUMBER: One of the most significant numbers in a numerology chart, derived from the individual's birth date. It represents their true essence, life purpose, and the path they are destined to follow.

MASTER NUMBER: The numbers 11, 22, and 33, which are believed to have a strong presence in the cosmos. They have the power to inspire and elevate life because each Master Number has twin digits that intensify its vibrations. Anyone with a Master Number as a Core Number is likely to have heightened intuition, potential, or intelligence.

MATURITY NUMBER: A number calculated using the birth date and shows the individual's potential for personal growth, wisdom, and fulfillment later in life.

NAME CHART: A numerological chart that examines the numeric influences present in an individual's full birth name. It typically includes the Expression Number, Character Number, and other relevant numbers derived from the name.

PAST LIFE: Also known as previous incarnation, this refers to previous lifetimes experienced before a soul's current incarnation.

PERSONAL DAY NUMBER: A number derived from an individual's birth date and represents specific traits and tendencies associated with that day of the month.

PERSONAL MONTH NUMBER: A number derived from an individual's birth date and represents specific traits and habits that will influence a particular month of an individual's life.

PERSONAL YEAR NUMBER: A number calculated to predict the theme, focus, and energy of a specific year in an individual's life. It is derived from your birth date and the current calendar year.

CHAPTER 1

Exploring the Numbers

· ·

BECAUSE NUMEROLOGY IS basically the study of numbers and their energetic influence in our lives, the best place to get started is to meet each number. Each number has a meaning that goes far beyond its mathematical value and can unlock insights into your character, your future, and even your purpose in life.

In Western numerology, numbers one through nine represent the basic components of existence. Each has a distinct vibration and symbolic meaning. Now here's a twist: For most numerological calculations, the number 10 doesn't really exist. Numerological calculations are performed by adding up all of the numbers in a string, over and over, until we get down to a single digit. The exception is the Master Numbers. The numbers 11, 22, and 33 are believed to have the power to inspire and elevate life because each Master Number has twin digits that intensify its vibrations. If you're calculating one of your Core Numbers and hit 11, 22, or 33, stop right there! There is no need to add those doubled-up digits to get a single one; claim that Master Number as your own.

Although these numbers represent broad archetypes, the ways they show up in your chart will determine how you should interpret them. Having 6 as your Inner Soul Number will mean something slightly different from having 6 as your Karmic Debt Number, as you'll soon learn. But before you create that chart and explore the relationships between your numbers, we'll introduce them as individual entities, one by one. They may also show up in your life as subtle nudges from the universe. If you start seeing a single digit or a string of digits everywhere—especially if they're any of the Master Numbers—that recurrence has significance! And familiarizing yourself with the profiles of these numbers can help you make sense of the numerological messages you're receiving.

NUMBER 1

FAMOUS 1 LIFE PATHS

Oscar de la Renta, Walt
Disney, Steve Jobs,
Martin Luther King Jr.,
George Washington,
Tiger Woods

The number 1 is all about fresh starts, opportunities, and the potential for growth because it symbolizes the energy of initiation and the spark of creation. This number is connected to singularity and the idea of taking the first step on a new journey. Makes sense, right?

This number appears in key chart positions for people who are self-reliant, assertive, and ambitious. They tend to have an innovative mindset, a strong sense of accomplishment, and outstanding leadership abilities. Because of their tenacity and self-assurance, they are natural innovators who inspire others to follow in their footsteps. (Think: the person who takes the reins in *every* group project they've ever been assigned.)

People with 1 in key chart positions have incredible capabilities, but they might also face some of the challenges that go along with independent-mindedness. Traits such as selfishness, impatience, and stubbornness can be part of their characters. By acknowledging and resolving these shortcomings, 1s may overcome obstacles with more self-awareness and balance.

THE NUMBER 1 IN DAILY LIFE

People with 1 in key chart positions seem endlessly able to take initiative, persevere in the face of challenges, and inspire people with their vision and charm. In everyday life, you'll see these folks following their passions and leaving a lasting impression on the world. And they do it as naturally as walking or breathing. They are independent thinkers who don't mind breaking away from the crowd and blazing their own trails to success.

The lessons of the number 1 are focused on bravery, self-acceptance, and self-discovery. People who are 1s frequently vibrate with originality, strength, leadership, and the capacity for independence, inspiring others to embrace their own individuality and increase their confidence.

THE NUMBER 1 AND TAROT

The tarot card most commonly associated with the number 1 is the Magician, and for many reasons. For starters, this is card 1 in the Major Arcana, the set of 22 powerful trump cards in a tarot deck. Most decks depict the Magician—who represents the connection between the spiritual and material realms—as a figure standing with one hand pointing toward the sky and the other pointing toward the earth. Willpower, leadership, manifestation, and control over the elements are all connected to the imposing figure of the Magician.

Just like the number 1, the Magician personifies the capacity to make ideas come to life and to harness inner energies to achieve goals and objectives. This archetype encourages individuals to recognize and discover their own talents and abilities, trust in their intuition, and take decisive action to manifest their desires.

When you find the number 1 in significant positions within your numerology chart, you are encouraged to embrace the traits of the Magician. You can harness the synergistic energies of the number and the card to attain personal development and success by aligning yourself with these characteristics.

THE NUMBER 1 WITHIN ASTROLOGY

The zodiac signs of Leo and Aries correspond with the characteristics of the number 1. Aries, the first sign of the zodiac, represents bravery, initiative, and a strong, outspoken character. And Leo, symbolized by the regal lion, radiates confidence, inventiveness, and a natural flair for leadership, all qualities that are aligned with the fundamentals of the number 1. Individuals who are born under these signs, or who have 1 in key chart positions, are frequently distinguished by their tenacity, vigor, and magnetic charm. They thrive in leadership roles and when they pursue their passions with bold enthusiasm.

If you have 1 in any key chart positions, you can harness the magnetic energy and leadership qualities associated with both the number 1 and the zodiac signs Aries and Leo. The influence of these signs will enhance the fact that you are particularly well-equipped to lead with confidence, take bold action, embrace creativity, pursue passions with enthusiasm, radiate magnetic charm, and show tenacity and determination. By recognizing and utilizing the synergy between the number 1 and the astrological influences of Aries and Leo, you can easily maximize your potential.

THE NUMBER 1 AND THE UNIVERSE

The birthstone for January (the first month of the year), the gemstone garnet, matches the assertive traits of the number 1 because it symbolizes power, courage, and passion. The sun embodies confidence, energy, and individuality, further amplifying shared characteristics with 1. And all hues of red—which is associated with the number 1, garnet, *and* the sun—stimulate action, bravery, and passion. They weave a beautiful tapestry of empowerment when combined.

These qualities are fueled even further by the sun's radiant energy, which also increases one's capacity for leadership and creativity. This bond is strengthened by the color red, which also inspires courage and a fiery personality. People are motivated to embrace their inner power, take bold risks with bravery, and lead with confidence and determination by this connection.

When people wear garnet, embrace the color red, and connect with solar energy, they can easily amplify their number 1 energy. You can do this by wearing garnet jewelry, wearing red clothing, spending time outdoors in the sunlight, using daily affirmations or visualizations, and by incorporating mindfulness or meditation practices. By consciously integrating these components into your daily life, you actively engage with and amplify the energies associated with the number 1.

MANTRA

"I balance."

KEY WORDS

Harmony, cooperation,
diplomacy,
intuition, empathy

FAMOUS 2 LIFE PATHS

Madonna,
Gwyneth Paltrow,
Ronald Reagan,
Emma Watson

As you might expect, because it's so strongly associated with partnerships and pairings, the number 2 resonates with cooperation, empathy, harmony, intuition, and diplomacy. It's always reflecting the duality found in nature; day and night, yin and yang, life and death. Because the number 2 resonates with sensitivity, intuition, and empathy, people with 2 in key chart positions are skilled at establishing relationships and sensing the feelings of others. Its power resides in its capacity to encourage harmony, resolve disputes, and enable clearer communication.

People who have 2 in key chart positions usually flourish in group settings and in careers that demand cooperation and finding common ground. They are skilled at listening with compassion, recognizing both sides of an issue, and identifying points of agreement. Their loving and nurturing personalities encourage a sense of support and belonging within communities.

That said, number 2s' inclination for diplomacy can occasionally lead to avoidance of confrontations, even important ones that merit their care and attention. Luckily, because these people are tenacious in their search for peace, when they finally *do* step into confrontation, they quickly find creative answers to their problems.

THE NUMBER 2 IN DAILY LIFE

The capacity to promote harmony and forge connections is one of 2's strengths. People with 2 in key chart positions are naturally gifted at cooperation, empathy, and diplomacy. They may act in a passive capacity as mediators or work in the background to create balance and harmony in situations or relationships. They are born peacekeepers.

Number 2s can be a positive influence on those around them by modeling listening and accepting differences to promote growth and connection among people. However, if this energy is not balanced, it may result in indecision, codependence, or passivity—an unwillingness to assert oneself. Peacekeeping can have a dark side if the person doing it can't enforce their own boundaries.

THE NUMBER 2 AND TAROT

The High Priestess is the tarot card that is most frequently associated with the number 2. The second card in the Major Arcana, she stands for the connection between the conscious and subconscious minds, and she is frequently shown as a lady seated between the worlds of light and darkness, signifying intuition and knowledge. The number 2 reminds us of the interconnectedness of opposites and the need to find harmony within ourselves and the world around us.

The High Priestess encourages people to follow their inner direction and explore the depths of their intuition. She is often linked to mystery, wisdom, and secret knowledge. This card and the number 2 both emphasize the value of inner knowledge and intuition, inspiring people to follow their gut instincts and embrace uncertainty, no matter how scary doing so may feel in the moment.

If you have 2 in any key chart positions, you can harness the energy of 2 and the archetype of the High Priestess to trust your intuition, seek balance and harmony, explore mysteries and hidden knowledge, embrace patience and sensitivity, meditate and reflect, and nurture relationships. By embracing these qualities and practices, you align yourself with the energies of both.

THE NUMBER 2 WITHIN ASTROLOGY

Because the number 2 is strongly linked to qualities such as collaboration and sensitivity, it has a natural affinity with Taurus and Cancer.

Venus rules the earth sign of Taurus, a sign that appreciates stability, loyalty, and nurturing bonds. People with a Taurus sun are noted for their dependability and steadfastness, traits that are consistent with the solidity and groundedness of the number 2.

The moon rules the sign of Cancer, which is known for its emotional depth, intuition, and nurturing tendencies. Like number 2, Cancer emphasizes the value of home, family, and emotional stability.

Relationships and emotional stability are important to both Taurus and Cancer, which aligns with the harmony and balance that the number 2 desires. This relationship highlights the significance of emotional receptivity, stability, and nurturing traits in both astrology and numerology.

If you have 2 in any key chart positions, you can harness the energy of the number 2, Taurus, and Cancer to cultivate strong relationships, embrace sensitivity and intuition, nurture emotional stability, foster harmony and balance, develop patience, and prioritize home and family. Whether in personal or professional surroundings, you can use this synergy to create a balanced and fulfilling life.

THE NUMBER 2 AND THE UNIVERSE

The moon is the planetary body that rules the number 2, and it represents emotions, the subconscious, and intuition. Its cyclical stages mirror life's tides and embody the polarity and duality ingrained in the number 2.

Moonstone's brilliant appearance and graceful energy are a wonderful match for the number 2's frequency. Moonstone enhances intuition, promotes emotional balance, and strengthens connections with divine feminine energy. Its connection with the moon intensifies its calming and relaxing properties, making it an effective tool for emotional healing and personal growth.

The colors orange, peach, and apricot—all of which inspire feelings of comfort, harmony, and inventiveness—mirror the energy of the number 2. The peaceful, comforting qualities of 2 are reflected in these colors, and in combination they can help foster emotional well-being and encourage cooperation and understanding in all relationships.

You can amplify the energy of the number 2 in your numerology chart by integrating moon-related practices, moonstone, and these colors into your daily life. Wearing moonstone jewelry or meditating with a piece of moonstone in your left hand can enhance your intuition. To tap into lunar energy, you can bathe under the moon to absorb its calming rays or track moon phases so you can align your daily activities with the moon. Finally, wearing shades of orange, peach, coral, or apricot or decorating your living space with these hues will evoke feelings of comfort and creativity.

NUMBER 3

MANTRA

"I create."

KEY WORDS

Creativity, communicative, optimism, sociability, expressive

FAMOUS 3 LIFE PATHS

Maya Angelou, Jimmy Buffett, Leonardo da Vinci, Kate Middleton, Katy Perry, J. K. Rowling, Barbara Walters

The number 3 is held sacred in many spiritual and religious contexts: the maiden, mother, and crone in Wicca; the holy trinity in Christianity; the three jewels of Buddhism. It's a number of tremendous power across many cultures. In numerology, 3 is a symbol for creativity, optimism, sociability, self-expression, and communication. It personifies the vibrant spirit of expansion and growth in the natural world, reflecting natural cycles of birth, growth, and fruition.

Individuals with 3 in key chart positions typically have lots of charm, optimism, and enthusiasm as well as a natural talent for storytelling. They often succeed in artistic pursuits, finding satisfaction from expressing themselves and sharing their unique perspectives with the world.

But it's not all passion and inspiration; the spontaneity and enthusiasm of the number 3 can occasionally result in disorganized energy, restlessness, or a tendency to overcommit. Luckily, 3s have a tremendous capacity for resiliency—the ability to pick themselves up after failure and turn every event into a learning opportunity.

THE NUMBER 3 IN DAILY LIFE

Most 3's have a special capacity to elevate, inspire, and bring joy to others. These folks can passively energize all undertakings and inspire people to share their unique talents and inspiration with the world. People with 3 in key chart positions lead by example.

The lessons of number 3 are to embrace creativity and enjoy the diversity of human experience in all social situations. This number is vibrationally associated with joy, growth, and self-expression. People who have 3 in key chart positions serve as a reminder for all of us to look for beauty, pleasure, and inspiration everywhere we go.

THE NUMBER 3 AND TAROT

The tarot card known as the Empress is typically associated with the number 3 in numerology. The third card in the Major Arcana, the Empress stands for the connection between the material and natural worlds and is frequently shown in green hues, sitting on a throne and surrounded by lush greenery. She is a representation of creativity, abundance, fertility, and the divine feminine spirit.

Both the number 3 and the Empress inspire people to express their unique talents and turn their dreams into reality. Both place a strong emphasis on the values of progress, creativity, and abundance and helping people have happy and fulfilled lives.

If you have 3 in any key chart positions, you can harness its energy and the archetype of the Empress to enhance your creativity, manifest abundance, connect with nature, enhance communication, engage in growth opportunities, and cultivate joy and optimism.

THE NUMBER 3 WITHIN ASTROLOGY

The number 3 represents growth, optimism, and a lively energy that seeks to explore the world with enthusiasm and curiosity. Sagittarius and Pisces are also associated with these attributes in the zodiac.

The archer is the symbol of Sagittarius, a sign recognized for its unbounded optimism, love of freedom, and spirit of adventure. Just like people with number 3 in key chart spots, those born under this sign are frequently philosophical, open-minded, and eager to discover new things.

Pisces is symbolized by the fish and associated with creativity, intuition, and a strong spiritual connection. People born under this sign are often sensitive, compassionate, and highly creative, aligning with the expressive and imaginative qualities of the number 3.

Together, these correlations paint a picture of those who are eager to express themselves creatively and embrace life's journey with optimism and wonder.

If you have 3 in any key chart positions, you can easily harness the combined energies of the number and these signs to enhance your life through embracing adventure and learning, expressing your creativity, maintaining optimism and open-mindedness, balancing freedom and responsibility, fostering emotional and spiritual growth, and engaging in community or social activities.

THE NUMBER 3 AND THE UNIVERSE

Jupiter is the planet most frequently linked to the number 3, which makes sense because they both express growth, optimism, and expansion. The warmth and vibrancy of the number 3 also resonate in all colors of yellow, bringing forth feelings of joy, inspiration, and optimism. The number 3 encourages people to express their thoughts, embrace their talents, and celebrate the abundance of life, as does the gemstone citrine. Jupiter, citrine, and yellow tones all support the imaginative, expressive, and gregarious qualities of the number 3, inspiring individuals to discover their goals and share their unique gifts with the world.

If you have 3 in any key chart positions, you can actively engage with the expansive and optimistic energies associated with Jupiter by studying its placement in your birth chart and consider how you can harness its optimistic and growth-oriented qualities. By wearing citrine jewelry or meditating with it, the crystals will amplify feelings of joy, inspiration, and abundance. Lastly, by surrounding yourself in yellow tones, either by wearing it or using it in décor, you can create an environment that fosters creativity and positivity.

NUMBER

4

MANTRA

"I build."

KEY WORDS

Stability, practicality, diligence, loyalty, organization

FAMOUS 4 LIFE PATHS

Beyoncé, Clint Eastwood, Bill Gates, Margaret Thatcher, Oprah Winfrey

The number 4 represents stability, structure, and practicality. It reflects the solid foundation observed in the natural world, including concepts such as the four elements (earth, air, fire, and water) and the four seasons. This number is associated with traits such as hard work, determination, and organization, reflecting the steady progress and strength found in nature's cycles.

While those individuals with the number 4 in key chart positions have exceptional strengths in structure and stability, they might grapple with qualities such as rigidity, stubbornness, or resistance to change. Still, steadfast 4s may overcome these obstacles through simple self-awareness. If they acknowledge and deal with their shortcomings, their capacity for hard work can win out.

THE NUMBER 4 IN DAILY LIFE

When it comes to jobs requiring meticulous preparation, perseverance, and attention to detail, 4s are a natural fit. In social situations, 4s can be found quietly influencing situations with dependable energy or encouraging the people around them to embrace hard work, determination, and practicality.

The lessons of 4 are rooted in responsibility. Everything about this number offers us a sense of security and grounding, encouraging us to build our lives on a solid foundation of integrity and determination. Fours are associated with dependability, self-control, and structure, helping people with this number in key chart positions lay the groundwork for future success.

THE NUMBER 4 AND TAROT

The fourth card in the Major Arcana is the Emperor, an archetype that's closely connected to the number 4. The Emperor is frequently depicted sitting on a sturdy throne with a scepter held in his arm. He is the embodiment of authority, accountability, and the creation of order in the tangible world while also reflecting the qualities of leadership, organization, and practicality.

The Emperor emphasizes the importance of discipline, responsibility, and authority in achieving goals and maintaining stability. Like the number 4, he supports a structured approach to life, establishing healthy boundaries, and exercising control over circumstances.

If you have 4 in any key chart positions, you can utilize the energy of the number and the archetype of the Emperor to establish structure and order, exercise leadership and authority, take accountability for your actions, and cultivate discipline and focus. By aligning yourself with the energies of 4 and the Emperor, you can create lasting impact in the world.

THE NUMBER 4 WITHIN ASTROLOGY

Both Capricorn and Aquarius share traits of practicality, determination, and a strong sense of responsibility with the number 4.

The Sea Goat, the symbol of Capricorn, reflects ambition, discipline, and a strong work ethic. Those born under this sign are often focused on building a solid foundation for themselves and others by working hard to reach their goals with determination and focus. This is in line with the number 4's methodical and grounded character, which emphasizes accountability and stability.

Aquarius, represented by the Water Bearer, is known for its innovative thinking, humanitarianism, and creativity. Individuals born under this sign are often independent, progressive, and drawn to movements that advance equality and social justice. This may not sound like a natural alignment at first, but the practical qualities of 4 enable them to bring their dreams of a better future to life.

If you have 4 in any key chart positions, you can bridge the connection between the number and the signs of Capricorn and Aquarius. You'll want to capitalize on practicality and determination, embrace responsibility and accountability, and build a solid foundation for change. By implementing these practices into your life, you can effectively harness the energies of both the number and its complementary zodiac signs.

THE NUMBER 4 AND THE UNIVERSE

The number 4's vibration emits steadiness, order, and practicality. People with 4 in key chart positions nearly always exude the qualities of diligence, self-control, and accountability, characteristics that are also reflected in Saturn, the number's ruling planet. Saturn also represents time, perseverance, and structure and emphasizes the need for discipline and accountability in achieving long-term goals.

The energy of the number 4 is usually matched with the gemstone jade. Jade—often referred to as the stone of luck and wealth—encourages abundance, balance, and harmony. Its alignment with Saturn intensifies its grounding and stabilizing qualities, helping maintain focus and perseverance when challenges arise.

All shades of green match the frequency of the number 4, which is often associated with growth, harmony, and renewal. Green hues evoke feelings of balance and stability, which then help create a sense of security and peace. This color echoes the logical and grounded characteristics of the number 4, supporting perseverance and advancement by concentrated effort.

If you have 4 in any key chart positions, you can actively engage with the energies associated with Saturn by developing effective time management skills to maximize productivity and by setting measurable goals. When you are working with jade, you should either meditate with it to connect to its positive vibration or carry it with you. Finally, you can wear all of the shades of green or consider decorating with green hues to enhance feelings of balance, stability, and renewal.

NUMBER 5

The number 5 is the embodiment of boundary-pushing, intelligence, communication, curiosity, and adventure. It illustrates how the natural world is always evolving, reflecting the never-ending cycles of growth, transformation, and renewal. The importance of living life to the fullest is underlined by the number 5, which is connected to the five human senses.

Individuals with number 5 in key chart positions are often adventurous, flexible, open-minded, and very resourceful, with a natural ability to flourish under a wide range of circumstances. They dominate in roles that require ingenuity and quick thinking and are unafraid to mold themselves to shifting circumstances. Although many people fear change, 5s welcome it as an opportunity for growth and discovery.

THE NUMBER 5 IN DAILY LIFE

Sometimes the number 5's love of excitement and variety can lead to restlessness or lack of focus, but its strength lies in its resilience and ability to acclimate to new circumstances with conviction and ease.

Passively, the number 5 shows up through the creative energy of development and transformation that quietly affects situations. People with this number in key chart positions enhance the experiences of others with their adventurous energy, urging those around them to embrace change and seek new opportunities for growth and discovery.

The lessons that 5s teach us revolve around making peace with change. This number urges us to embrace all of life's diverse experiences, to find excitement in the unknown, and to remain open-minded and flexible no matter what our journeys may bring.

THE NUMBER 5 AND TAROT

The Hierophant in tarot and the number 5 are connected through shared themes of personal transformation, guidance, and spiritual exploration. The fifth card in the Major Arcana, the Hierophant is a figure of authority who is frequently shown as a religious or spiritual leader decked out in elaborate ceremonial robes. He is a guide and a teacher, a shaman who passes along the lessons of natural law, linking him to 5's affinity for cycles of transformation.

The Hierophant is linked to tradition, spiritual understanding, and the pursuit of deeper meanings. Both this archetype and the number 5 encourage us to seek guidance from established teachings and spiritual authorities.

If you have 5 in any key chart positions, you can actively engage with the archetype energies of the Hierophant and the number by deepening your spiritual journey, expanding your consciousness with meditation, and sharing your spiritual wisdom with others.

THE NUMBER 5 WITHIN ASTROLOGY

The number 5 represents adventure, adaptability, and freedom—qualities that are also reflected in the signs of Virgo and Gemini.

The twins represent Gemini, a zodiac sign known for its curiosity, flexibility, and communication skills. People born under this sign are often intellectually curious, sociable, and quick-witted. They also seek out excitement and diversity in their life, just as the number 5 reflects adaptability and flexibility.

Virgo is symbolized by the virgin, and people born under this sign are known for their practicality, attention to detail, and analytical approach to life. Although Virgo may seem more grounded than Gemini, when its energy merges with that of the number 5, the result is a sense of versatility and adaptability along with excitement around change and exploring new possibilities.

You can readily use the energies associated with Virgo, Gemini, and the number 5 if you have 5 in any key chart positions. You will be able to embrace intellectual curiosity, cultivate flexibility and adaptability, embrace diversity and excitement, balance practicality with exploration, find practical solutions, and easily communicate and connect to others when you actively engage with the synergistic energy of these three entities.

THE NUMBER 5 AND THE UNIVERSE

The energy of 5 encourages people to be curious and pursue intellectual stimulation while embracing new experiences. Mercury—the planet that rules communication, intelligence, and movement—has a natural connection to the number 5. Mercury enhances mental dexterity and encourages clear communication, which gives rise to new knowledge and fearless exploration.

A stone known for its peaceful blue-green hues, aquamarine is in perfect harmony with the vibration of the number 5. And aquamarine's natural traits are enhanced by its association with Mercury, which facilitates decision-making and fosters mental clarity during periods of change.

The energy of the number 5 aligns perfectly with the colors light blue, turquoise, and aqua, which evoke emotions of openness, creativity, and tranquility. These calming colors promote creativity, self-expression, and the endless possibilities that come so easily to number 5s.

There are actionable steps to strengthen the connection between the number 5, Mercury, the gemstone aquamarine, and all the hues of light blue. Mercury is known for its impact over communication, so by practicing active listening and expressing yourself clearly, you'll easily engage with Mercury's influence. Wearing the gemstone aquamarine or meditating with it will promote mental clarity and inspire fearless exploration. Incorporating light blue, turquoise, and aqua tones into your environment or wearing these colors can create a sense of calm and tranquility. Allow these influences to guide you on a journey of self-discovery, growth, and adventure.

NUMBER 6

KEY WORDS

Compassionate, protective, nurturing, responsible, loving

FAMOUS 6 LIFE PATHS

Johann Sebastian Bach, Emily Dickinson, Audrey Hepburn, Christopher Reeve, Eleanor Roosevelt

The number 6 is imbued with the energy of trustworthiness, empathy, caregiving, and balance. It symbolizes the nurturing traits seen in the natural world, reflecting the protection that parents and guardians offer to their young in all animal kingdoms. People with 6 in key chart positions frequently have a strong emphasis on family, community, and service, which highlights how crucial social ties and relationships are to creating harmony and balance in life.

When compared to other numbers, 6s are the most caring and empathetic. They are appreciated for their capacity to foster peace and togetherness in all that surrounds them, and they stand out in careers involving mentorship, dependability, and giving assistance to others.

THE NUMBER 6 IN DAILY LIFE

People with 6 in key chart positions should know that their emphasis on nurturing others might occasionally cause them to become overprotective or neglect their own needs. Their true power resides in creating a secure and encouraging atmosphere where others can flourish.

An innate propensity for nurturing and healing of all natural living forms is something 6s do passively, almost without thinking. Most 6s live out values such as empathy, accountability, compassion, and love by creating nurturing circumstances where others may easily thrive. The lessons that 6 brings us revolve around the importance of nurturing relationships, fostering empathy, and embracing responsibility.

THE NUMBER 6 AND TAROT

The number 6 overflows with compassion, love, and balance, the same themes depicted in the Lovers card in tarot. The sixth card in the Major Arcana, the Lovers symbolize the union of opposites, such as masculine and feminine energies, or the peaceful fusion of opposites within oneself. Both the card and the number represent relationships, choices, and the interconnectedness of individuals. The number 6 fosters unity and is reflected in the union depicted on the Lovers card.

Like the Lovers, the number 6 encourages people to make decisions based on love, compassion, and harmony. It signifies the importance of partnerships, whether romantic or platonic, in achieving balance and fulfillment with both parties.

If you have 6 in any key chart positions, you can utilize the energies associated with the Lovers card and the number to cultivate deeper connections in your relationships and achieve greater balance in your life. You can do this by expressing gratitude, following your heart, nurturing loving connections, finding inner balance, practicing empathy, celebrating diversity, balancing harmonious connections, letting go of resentment, and communicating with compassion.

THE NUMBER 6 WITHIN ASTROLOGY

The number 6 is beautifully aligned with the signs Taurus and Libra because all three are associated with harmony, balance, and nurturing energy.

Taurus, represented by the bull, is a sign that values security, sensuality, and a close bond with Earth. People born under this sign typically value stability and comfort in their lives and are realistic, dependable, and grounded. This is consistent with the number 6's caring and nurturing qualities.

The scales symbolize Libra, a sign recognized for its tactfulness, equity, and focus on collaborations. People with Libra as their sun sign are frequently outgoing, diplomatic, and strive for harmony in both their personal and professional lives. Because 6 encourages balance and empathy, it enables Libras to handle relationships with tact and understanding.

The attributes of the number 6 are best represented by Taurus and Libra together, highlighting the significance of harmony, balance, and nurturing in interpersonal and social interactions.

You can harness the energies associated with Taurus, Libra, and the number 6 to cultivate deeper connections in your relationships and promote greater harmony in your life if you have a 6 in any key chart positions. To do this, you will need to embrace stability and security, cultivate collaboration and diplomacy, prioritize relationships and connections, promote self-care and emotional well-being, and create beauty and comfort.

THE NUMBER 6 AND THE UNIVERSE

Embodying the virtues of domesticity, love, and family, the number 6 urges people to build peaceful, harmonious relationships. Venus—the planet that rules love, beauty, and pleasure—is also linked to the number 6. Its impact raises the vibration of 6, encouraging creative expression, emotional connection, and a profound sense of beauty.

Rose quartz, sometimes referred to as the stone of unconditional love, aligns with the energy of 6s. It emits vibrations that encourage forgiveness, self-acceptance, and compassion. And to complete the circle, rose quartz's qualities are enhanced by its association with Venus, which promotes deep love and profound emotional healing.

The frequency of the number 6 resonates with the hues violet and indigo, both of which enhance intuition and spirituality. These colors are in harmony with the loving and compassionate qualities of the number 6 because they inspire introspection, emotional balance, and a closer bond with oneself and others.

You can easily engage with the energies associated with Venus, rose quartz, and violet and indigo hues to cultivate deeper connections in your relationships and promote emotional healing and balance in your life if you have a 6 in any key chart positions. Do this by surrounding yourself with beauty and harmony in your environment, wearing or meditating with the gemstone rose quartz (which will remind you of the importance of unconditional love and self-acceptance), and decorating with or wearing hues of indigo or violet. All of these actions will allow you to tap into your intuition and inner wisdom.

NUMBER
7

MANTRA

"I seek."

KEY WORDS

Perceptive, intellectual, analytical, introspective, spiritual

FAMOUS 7 LIFE PATHS

Princess Diana, John F. Kennedy, Bruce Lee, Elon Musk, William Shakespeare, Nikola Tesla

Another number that holds meaning in diverse spiritual traditions and mythologies, 7 shows up in sacred geometry in the seed of life; in the Bible multiple times, including the deadly sins and the number of days it took to create the world; as the number of chakras in the body; and in various forms across Islam, Buddhism, Judaism, and Hinduism. The number 7 is often associated with qualities such as perceptiveness, intellectuality, analytical thinking, introspection, and spirituality. It encourages people to investigate life's secrets and pursue spirituality as a means of enlightenment.

Due to their broad viewpoints and analytical nature, people who have 7 in key chart positions are typically skilled at seeing patterns, evaluating data, and exploring the depths of their own minds. They have strong intuition and sharp minds, which enable them to solve difficult riddles and unearth secrets. Most 7s naturally connect with their inner knowledge and spiritual direction because of their introspective character, which promotes personal growth and self-discovery.

THE NUMBER 7 IN DAILY LIFE

There's a lot to love about 7, but this number has its challenges, too. That propensity for spirituality and reflection can sometimes lead to a tendency to retreat from society or self-isolate. To keep their lives in balance, people with 7 in key chart positions must learn to temper their secretive tendencies.

The passive presence of 7s will impact perceptions and insights, supporting people in times of reflection, contemplation, and introspection. This number inspired people to ponder life's mysteries and dive into their inner selves.

THE NUMBER 7 AND TAROT

Perseverance, tenacity, and success are common motifs shared by the Chariot in tarot and the number 7. The Chariot card, seventh in the Major Arcana, shows a person riding a chariot drawn by two sphinxes, signifying victory over adversaries and the path to prosperity. Just as 7s signify cognitive endeavors, critical thinking, and spiritual exploration, the Chariot represents the inner strength and resilience required to overcome obstacles and achieve goals.

The Chariot and the number 7 both encourage people to channel their inner motivation and concentrate their efforts on a certain purpose or goal. Together, they represent the values of self-discipline and determination, encouraging the capacity to rise above hardship with inner strength and focused intention.

If you have 7 in any key chart positions, you may use the Chariot card's energies of tenacity and success by viewing obstacles as chances for personal development. Use your inner strength and critical-thinking abilities to overcome hurdles with tenacity and resolve, knowing that every setback is a step closer to your goals. Have faith in your capacity to withstand hardship, maintain your course of action, and let your resolve carry you to success. Accept the road of introspection and spiritual learning, understanding that each event advances your own development.

THE NUMBER 7 WITHIN ASTROLOGY

Deeply perceptive water signs Pisces and Cancer have a special bond with the esoteric number 7. This number is associated with contemplation, spirituality, and inner wisdom, traits that are also common to both astrological signs.

Pisces, the dreamy empath, resonates with the depths of the subconscious, often drawn to spiritual endeavors and mystical encounters. This otherworldliness complements 7's introspective nature.

Similarly, Cancer—led by intuition and emotional depth—finds comfort in nurturing others and exploring the depths of the soul, reflecting the truth-seeking nature of 7.

When combined, Pisces and Cancer represent the introspective and intuitive parts of 7, and people who can leverage the energies of all three will skillfully navigate the emotional tides of life.

The amethyst crystal, known for its ability to strengthen intuition, promote spiritual growth, and facilitate deep meditation is vibrationally similar to the number 7. Both resonate with the energy of introspection, mysticism, and intellectual explorations.

Neptune—planet of dreams, intuition, and the subconscious mind—is the planet most often associated with the number 7. The influence of Neptune inspires people to delve into their inner selves and embrace the search for meaning.

The most common hues linked with the number 7 are violet and deep purple, which evoke enlightenment, knowledge, and spirituality. Violet and purple both arouse the imagination, promote spiritual development, and inspire people to accept their inner wisdom and trust their intuition.

The vibration, crystal, planet, and color of the number 7 all work together to help forge a deeper understanding of and connection to the universe.

If you have 7 in any key chart positions, you can engage with the energies associated with the amethyst crystal, Neptune, and the colors violet and deep purple to deepen your connection to the universe and enhance your spiritual journey. Harness intuitive insights and facilitate deep meditation when you use amethyst while meditating or by wearing the gemstone among your jewelry. Neptune's influential energy can be utilized by exploring dreamwork and enhancing your intuition. By embracing the colors of violet and deep purple, you can cultivate spiritual awareness and tap into creative inspiration. Allow these influences to guide you as you explore the mysteries of the universe and uncover the hidden truths of your soul.

MANTRA

"I manifest."

KEY WORDS

Abundance, ambition, achievement, authority, success

FAMOUS 8 LIFE PATHS

Amelia Earhart, Henry Ford, Stephen Hawking, Nelson Mandela, Martha Stewart

In the natural world, due to its symmetrical design and infinite loop, 8 is frequently connected to the concepts of balance and infinity. Patterns of 8 appear in seedpods, spiderwebs, and snowflakes, echoing throughout many forms of life and matter. This number's geometric properties lend it stability, symmetry, and resilience.

The power of the number 8 is in its practical and disciplined approach to work along with its unwavering drive to achieve goals. People with 8 in key chart positions are frequently natural leaders who can handle difficult situations through decisiveness and strategic thinking. They are driven by a desire for success and accomplishment and have a strong sense of responsibility.

Despite their strengths, 8s may also have a tendency toward workaholism and an excessive focus on monetary gain at the price of their own well-being. Their authoritative character can sometimes result in thought processes that are inflexible and rigid.

THE NUMBER 8 IN DAILY LIFE

The number 8's focus on abundance, ambition, and authority can manifest both actively and passively in a variety of contexts. It ignites people's goals, which gives them a sense of authority and leadership, and actively pushes them toward success and achievement.

The three key teachings of the number 8 are balance, perseverance, and discipline. This number is imbued with ambition and prosperity, and people who have charts filled with 8s are often wildly successful. This admirable quality can also go too far, possibly leading to a compulsion to work or an obsession with accumulating wealth.

The vibe of the number 8 is one of strength and manifestation, inspiring people to take control of their lives and realize their innate potential.

THE NUMBER 8 AND TAROT

In both tarot and numerology, the number 8 is closely linked to themes of strength, resilience, and inner power. The eighth card in the Major Arcana, Strength depicts a figure taming a lion through gentle yet firm control, symbolizing the mastery of one's primal instincts and the ability to overcome challenges through inner courage and resilience. This card encourages people to harness their inner strength, patience, and compassion to navigate life's obstacles with grace and integrity, guidance that 8 also provides.

The ability to wield power wisely is strongly emphasized in both the Strength card and the number 8. Both encourage people to face challenges head-on with poise and confidence.

If you have 8 in any key chart positions, you can tap into the energies associated with both the Strength card in tarot and the number to navigate challenges and achieve success in your life. Actively engage with these energies by cultivating inner strength, embracing adversity, practicing self-confidence, exercising patience and compassion, and practicing mindfulness. Harness your personal power by setting clear intentions and taking action, and continuously seeking guidance and support by connecting with mentors.

NUMBER 8 WITHIN ASTROLOGY

Neighboring signs of the zodiac Capricorn and Aquarius are both in tune with the potent energy of the number 8. All of them resonate with authority, ambition, and innovation.

Capricorn, the disciplined achiever, embodies the structured approach to success often associated with the number 8. Ruled by Saturn, the planet of responsibility and discipline, Capricorn eagerly climbs the ladder of achievement under the direction of a sense of purpose, reflecting the ambition and authority of the number 8.

On the other hand, Aquarius's creative spirit and unique outlook on life offers a different perspective on the energy of 8. Aquarius aspires to disrupt the current status quo by pushing limits and embracing change, under the guidance of Uranus, the planet of rebellion and progress.

Capricorn and Aquarius work together to forge their paths to prosperity and the advancement of society by utilizing the powerful force of 8.

If you have 8 in any key chart positions, you can draw upon the energies associated with both Capricorn and Aquarius to achieve success and make meaningful contributions to society. In order to utilize these energies you will need to embrace structure and discipline by setting defined goals with clarity, cultivating determination and ambition by staying focused on those goals, and embracing change and innovation by thinking outside the box. By integrating the energies of Capricorn and Aquarius, you can harness the potent force of the number 8 to achieve your goals, make a positive impact on society, and leave a lasting legacy of success and innovation.

THE NUMBER 8 AND THE UNIVERSE

Saturn, the ruling planet of the number 8, is also associated with responsibility, order, and karmic lessons. Its impact raises the vibration of the number 8, promoting self-control, perseverance, and the accomplishment of long-term objectives.

Black tourmaline, a protective gemstone, connects with and amplifies 8's energy. It eliminates negative energy while supporting inner strength and resilience. In addition, black tourmaline's properties are heightened through its relationship with Saturn; the stone provides stability and protection during challenging or transitional times.

The colors light brown and black resonate with the frequency of the number 8, arousing feelings of stability, strength, and anchoring. These colors go well with the authoritative and ambitious qualities of the number 8, encouraging people to take control of their lives, be more practical, and stand tall in their confidence.

If you have 8 in any key chart positions, you can engage with the energies associated with Saturn, black tourmaline, and the colors light brown and black. Saturn governs themes of responsibility, discipline, and structure; by harnessing these energies you'll be able to set appropriate boundaries when needed and practice time management. You can seek stabilization and protection by bringing black tourmaline into your space and by surrounding yourself with the colors of light brown, gray, and black.

NUMBER 9

MANTRA

"I serve."

KEY WORDS

Humanitarian, transformative, enlightened, philanthropic, harmonious

FAMOUS 9 LIFE PATHS

Jim Carrey, Bob Marley, Elvis Presley, Mother Teresa

The number 9 represents a complex web of deep values, including the completion of cycles, the fullness of life, and the interconnectedness of all living beings. This number has long been associated with spiritual awakening and enlightenment, signifying the conclusion of internal exploration and the achievement of a higher level of understanding. It resonates with wholeness, oneness, and universal love.

People with 9 at key places in their charts have a strong commitment to humanitarian issues and are motivated by a desire to improve society and lessen suffering. They are unmatched in their capacity to promote peace in interpersonal relationships and communities because they are living examples of collaboration and unity.

Although the number 9 has many advantages, it can also spark internal struggles. That strong idealistic perspective sometimes eclipses the harshness of reality, leading 9s to ignore important warning signs. Luckily 9's ultimate power comes from its ability to inspire positive change and a more compassionate and peaceful society.

THE NUMBER 9 IN DAILY LIFE

The number 9 frequently shows itself in the form of humanitarian gestures, transformative endeavors, and harmonious resolutions. Its lessons are about empathic behavior, selflessness, and acceptance of change. The vibrations of this number encourage people to accept new beginnings and to let go of the past.

However, because of its passive character, people may become complacent or turn to escapism to avoid dealing with challenging situations or disputes. Selflessness, compassion, and flexibility are among its best qualities, but self-neglect and avoiding responsibility are the dark underbelly of this number. In the end, 9 inspires people to live up to the greatest aspirations of humanity and work toward a more peaceful and enlightened way of life.

THE NUMBER 9 AND TAROT

There is a strong affinity between the Hermit card and the number 9, which both represent introspection, wisdom, and spiritual enlightenment. The ninth card in the Major Arcana, the Hermit features a lone man standing atop a mountain with a lamp in hand. This artwork is symbolic of the isolative path of self-realization and seeking inner truth, similar to the transformative power of 9.

The Hermit and the number 9 both stress the value of introspection and isolation as means of achieving deep insight and profound understanding. As the Hermit withdraws from the world to explore the depths of spirituality, the number 9 invites people to welcome the wisdom gained through introspection. When combined, they represent a path of self-exploration that leads to increased understanding, compassion, and harmony with the universe.

If you have 9 in any key chart positions, you can harness its energy and the energy of the Hermit by accepting periods of reflection and seclusion, allowing yourself the time and space to delve deep into your inner world. Meditation, journaling, and contemplative practices can aid in connecting with your inner knowledge and intuition. It may also be helpful to look for mentors or spiritual leaders who may provide direction and encouragement on your path of self-discovery. Keep in mind following your intuition and inner direction as you travel the path to spiritual enlightenment and personal development.

THE NUMBER 9 WITHIN ASTROLOGY

Though they do so in vastly different ways, Aries and Scorpio both work harmoniously with the number 9. The first sign of the zodiac, Aries represents qualities of boldness, independence, and initiative. This sign's pioneering energy is also reflected in 9, which evokes transition, the end of cycles, and the ambition needed to start new adventures.

Scorpio, on the other hand, is connected to transformation, depth, and intensity. Because 9 stands for enlightenment and harmony, it's a good match for Scorpio's drive to explore life's secrets. Scorpio's path of self-discovery frequently results in significant changes, mirroring 9's transformational qualities.

In both cases, the number 9 serves as a symbol of growth, progress, and the culmination of experiences, resonating strongly with the adventurous spirit of Aries and the transformative journey of Scorpio.

If you have 9 in any key chart positions, you can actively harness its energies by integrating the qualities of Aries and Scorpio into your life. From Aries, embrace the qualities of boldness, independence, and taking initiative. Use the pioneering energy of Aries to fuel your ambition and start new adventures fearlessly. Take the initiative in pursuing your goals and aspirations, and don't be afraid to step out of your comfort zone to explore new opportunities. From Scorpio, tap into the energies of transformation, depth, and intensity. Allow yourself to delve deep into your inner world and explore life's mysteries with curiosity and determination. Embrace the process of self-discovery and be open to significant changes and growth along the way.

THE NUMBER 9 AND THE UNIVERSE

The anchoring and stabilizing qualities of red jasper help it harmonize with the transformational energy of the number 9. Both encourage inner strength and bravery in times of change.

Mars—the planet of activity, energy, and assertiveness—is a fantastic match for 9's forward-thinking and energetic vibe. Mars's planetary influence inspires people to pursue their objectives with determination and passion, mirroring 9's commitment to revolutionary projects and humanitarian causes.

The action and passion of Mars and 9's dynamic nature work seamlessly with dark red, maroon, and crimson, all hues that symbolize energy and determination.

If you have 9 in any key chart positions, you can actively utilize the energies of red jasper, Mars, and the dynamic colors of dark red, maroon, and crimson to enhance your sense of inner strength, bravery, and determination. Carry or wear red jasper to anchor and stabilize your energy during times of change and transformation. Allow its grounding properties to provide you with the courage and resilience needed to navigate through challenges with grace and confidence. Integrate Mars's energy to take decisive action toward your goals, mirroring the commitment to creative projects and humanitarian causes associated with the number 9. Surround yourself with the dynamic colors of dark red, maroon, and crimson to invoke feelings of energy and determination.

Incorporate these colors into your environment through clothing or décor to enhance your sense of motivation and drive.

 ## WHERE IS NUMBER 10?

Soon you will learn how numerological calculations are made, but you'll need a little preview to understand why there's no entry for 10 in this chapter. Numerology focuses on single digits 1 through 9 and the three Master Numbers 11, 22, and 33. Most calculations are made by adding the numbers in a name or date together until they're down to a single digit. So 10 is 1 + 0 = 1.

If this is confusing now, don't worry. It'll make way more sense in the coming chapters.

MASTER NUMBER 11

MANTRA

"I inspire."

KEY WORDS

Intuitive, inspirational, spiritual, sensitive, influential

FAMOUS 11 LIFE PATHS

Bill Clinton, Michael Jordan, Barack Obama, Prince William

Master Number 11 is a symbol of harmony and balance in the natural world, signifying the coming together of opposites and the potential of achieving spiritual enlightenment. This number is like a bridge that connects the spiritual and material worlds. (Quick reminder Master Numbers are considered the nearly completed and fully realized traits of the single digits they add up to; in this case, number 2.)

Because of Master Number 11's depth of spiritual resonance, ability to inspire, and link to intuitive abilities, people with 11 in key chart positions are often perceptive and serve as beacons of light for others who are traveling a spiritual path. Their sensitivity enables them to connect with people intimately and empathetically, which inspires positive change and growth. Their capacity to activate others around them by creating feelings of unity and purpose makes them highly influential.

Occasionally this increased sensitivity can result in emotional overload or self-doubt, making it difficult to stay balanced. Even yet, 11s' spiritual awareness and intuitive abilities continue to be powerful assets that lead them and others toward enlightenment and deeper understanding.

THE NUMBER 11 IN DAILY LIFE

The intuitive, inspirational, and spiritual aspects of 11 come through in subtle ways, such as synchronistic events, epiphanies, and unexpected nudges from the universe. In action, those who have this number in key chart positions uplift others with their visionary ideas, guidance, and spiritual wisdom.

Master Number 11's teachings center on accepting spiritual development, learning to lead, and acting as a conduit for greater awareness. It's considered the most intuitive number of all by many experts, and it tends to appear in the charts of people with incredible imaginative powers. Its vices, however, sometimes surface as escapism, self-doubt, or a tendency toward impractical idealism.

THE NUMBER 11 AND TAROT

The concepts of truth, fairness, and balance are shared by Master Number 11 and the tarot card Justice. The eleventh card in the Major Arcana, the Justice card is depicted as a figure holding scales. It signifies the need for impartiality and ethical decision-making. Similarly, 11 represents the quest for enlightenment and truth.

Both Justice and Master Number 11 emphasize the importance of integrity and responsibility. They urge people to strive for balance in their actions and decisions, understanding that every choice carries consequences. Additionally, when faced with difficulties, they both encourage people to turn to their inner wisdom and intuition.

If you have 11 in any key chart positions, you can assimilate the energies of the Justice card and the Master Number by seeking truth and clarity, making ethical choices, practicing fairness, and aligning yourself with universal laws. By integrating these principles into your life, you can harness the powerful energies of Master Number 11 and the Justice card, encouraging a path of enlightenment, integrity, and balanced living.

THE NUMBER 11 WITHIN ASTROLOGY

Master Number 11 is linked to Aquarius and Pisces because all three share the qualities of enhanced spiritual awareness, intuitive abilities, and visionary thinking.

The humanitarian sign of the zodiac, Aquarius, represents the principles of harmony and progress and is frequently motivated by creative thinking and a desire to bring about constructive social change. Aquarius's ability to see outside the box and create new opportunities for the collective is amplified by 11's energy.

Similarly, Pisces, the empathic dreamer, is highly attuned to the emotional changes of the universe. Under the influence of Master Number 11, Pisces has an increase in spiritual depth and sensitivity, which may lead to profound connections with the divine and the capacity to direct creativity and compassion into transformative ventures.

If you have 11 in any key chart positions, you can use the energies of Aquarius and Pisces, combined with the Master Number, to leverage your intuition, pursue humanitarian goals, embrace creative thinking, set proper boundaries, and seek knowledge and growth. By integrating these practices, you can utilize the powerful energies of Aquarius, Pisces, and Master Number 11 to enhance your spiritual journey, contribute to the greater good, and manifest your visionary ideas into reality.

THE NUMBER 11 AND THE UNIVERSE

A strong link to the higher planes of awareness is reflected in the frequency of Master Number 11. Interestingly, Uranus—the planet of invention, rebellion, and sudden change—is correlated with the energy and nonconformist thinking of 11, inspiring people to embrace their individuality and spark change.

Silver, a color symbolizing intuition, mystery, and introspection, harmonizes with the 11's graceful qualities, suggesting a sense of clarity and openness to spiritual guidance.

Labradorite, a gemstone renowned for its iridescent hues and intuitive properties, resonates with 11's intuitive wisdom, enhancing psychic abilities and facilitating spiritual development.

Together, the planetary influence of Uranus, the color silver, and labradorite form a harmonious combination that amplifies Master Number 11's vibration, enabling people to tap into their inner guidance and to bring those lofty ideas into life.

If you have 11 in any key chart positions, you can actively use the influences of Uranus, the color silver, and labradorite to enhance your intuitive abilities, embrace your individuality, and bring about meaningful change. Tap into the energy of the planet Uranus to think outside of the box and embrace your unique perspective. By surrounding yourself with silver or wearing it, you can eliminate mental chatter, thus promoting introspection and self-reflection. Wearing or using the crystal labradorite will amplify your intuitive abilities and facilitate spiritual development.

MANTRA

"I master."

KEY WORDS

Visionary, ambitious, practical, mastery, strategic

FAMOUS 22 LIFE PATHS

Richard Branson,
14th Dalai Lama,
Paul McCartney,
Matthew McConaughey,
Dale Earnhardt

Master Number 22 amplifies ambition, practicality, and strategic thinking. This is a number of extraordinary potential. In nature, 22 shows up in numerous ways, often reflecting patterns of balance, symmetry, and completion. A classic example is the structure of human DNA, which consists of 22 pairs of chromosomes.

People who have 22 in key chart positions have an unmatched ability to think creatively and strategically; they can execute on big, far-reaching ideas with accuracy and practicality. This enables 22s to handle opportunities and resources effectively, even in the face of complicated circumstances.

Although there are many positives associated with Master Number 22, the intense pressure to excel can also lead to some challenges. The relentless pursuit of perfection can sometimes lead to feeling overwhelmed or burned out as a result of living up to such high standards. However, the advantages of Master Number 22 greatly exceed the disadvantages, making it a source of inspiration for those who have the courage to dream big and pursue their goals with unflinching dedication.

THE NUMBER 22 IN DAILY LIFE

This number bestows upon people a feeling of visionary potential and practical knowledge; it typically shows itself subtly but persistently. For people with 22 in key chart positions, it encourages bold ventures and calculated preparation, assisting them in realizing their highest goals and aspirations. Its vibration is in tune with the forces of transformation and long-term success, inspiring people to embrace their inner visions and follow their objectives with determination and strategic insight.

The dark side of Master Number 22 might take the form of excessive ambition or a tendency toward perfectionism, which makes people take on more than they can manage or become overly judgmental. All things considered, the Master Number 22 holds great promise for both individual and societal progress because it combines a strong dose of practical knowledge, imaginative thinking, and transformational power.

THE NUMBER 22 AND TAROT

The Fool card in tarot is a symbol for innocence, new beginnings, and the soul's journey. The 22nd card in the Major Arcana, it shows a carefree young person carrying a tiny bag, representing the beginning of a journey, free from the burdens of expectations or prior experiences. A powerful card, it embodies a sense of spontaneity, curiosity, and trust in the universe's guidance.

The Fool assumes greater significance when connected to Master Number 22, signifying the beginning of a spiritual quest toward enlightenment and mastery. This number enhances the Fool's potential, inspiring people to embrace their inner visions and take a fearless, faith-filled step into the unknown.

If you have 22 in any key chart positions, you can harness the combined energies of the Fool card and the Master Number by taking bold steps and staying open-minded, by trusting the universe, by following your intuition and practicing mindfulness, and by harnessing your inner vision and dreaming big.

THE NUMBER 22 WITHIN ASTROLOGY

Because Master Number 22 resonates with the traits of ambition, mastery, and transforming force, it's only natural that it would be closely linked to Capricorn and Scorpio.

The sign of Capricorn, which stands for ambition, self-control, and practicality, complements this number's emphasis on attaining measurable success and long-lasting achievements. Like the energy of 22, people born under the sign of Capricorn are frequently motivated by a strong desire for accomplishment and are prepared to work hard to achieve their goals.

In contrast, Scorpio is associated with intensity, depth, and transformation. Those born under this sign are frequently led to introspection in order to reach their greatest potential. Master Number 22 enhances Scorpio's natural capacity for significant personal transformation, inspiring people to tap into their inner strength and bring their greatest desires to life.

If you have 22 in any key chart positions, you can utilize the combined energies of Capricorn and Scorpio to achieve extraordinary success and personal transformation. In order to leverage Capricorn's energy, you'll need to level up your ambition and practicality by setting clear goals and committing to some hard work. Integrating and using Scorpio's energy requires you to tap into transformative power by embracing change and diving deep into introspection. By integrating the ambitious and practical nature of Capricorn with the transformative and intense qualities of Scorpio, and channeling the masterful energy of Number 22, you can achieve significant and lasting success.

THE NUMBER 22 AND THE UNIVERSE

Pluto, the planet associated with deep transformation, corresponds with 22's transformative power, which leads people toward significant personal growth and regeneration.

The frequency of the Master Number 22 is harmonized by lapis lazuli, a bright blue gemstone valued for enhancing intuition, wisdom, and spiritual insight.

The color gold symbolizes abundance, success, and divine illumination, resonating with 22's qualities of achievement, ambition, and mastery. Pluto, lapis lazuli, and gold combine to create a harmonious synergy that raises the vibration of the number 22, enabling people to accept transformation, connect with their inner wisdom, and bring their greatest desires to life.

If you have 22 in any key chart positions, you can actively harness the transformative energies of Pluto, lapis lazuli, and gold to propel yourself toward significant personal growth and achievement. When you fully embrace Pluto's transformational power, you'll be able to release the past and tap into your inner power more easily. Wearing lapis lazuli jewelry or carrying a piece of it will not only deepen your intuition, but it will also help you unlock spiritual insights and calm your mind. If you wear the color gold or wear gold jewelry, doing so will help you manifest success and illuminate your path.

MANTRA

"I teach."

KEY WORDS

Teacher, compassionate, wisdom, creative, influential

FAMOUS 33 LIFE PATHS

Thomas Edison,
Albert Einstein,
Stephen King,
John Lennon,
Meryl Streep

Master Number 33 symbolizes the pinnacle of spiritual enlightenment and the ability to convey divine wisdom and unconditional love in everyday life. It's considered to be the most authoritative number, even compared to the other Master Numbers 11 and 22, because it is the sum of both these numbers. People with 33 in key chart positions assume the role of the master teacher or spiritual guide.

Master Number 33s are endowed with a deep sense of creativity, knowledge, and compassion. They are called to guide and mentor others, inspiring positive transformation and growth. These rare people are powerful leaders and healers in their communities because of their capacity for profound empathy and loving advice.

THE NUMBER 33 IN DAILY LIFE

Master Number 33 shows up passively as a subtle yet profound influence, instilling people with a desire to find a path to higher service. When put into practice, this number encourages acts of selflessness, mentorship, and creative expression, guiding individuals toward fulfilling their life's purpose as teachers and healers.

The values of wisdom, compassion, and selflessness are central to the teachings of 33, which encourage people to live as manifestations of the divine. Its vibration encourages people to use their abilities for the benefit of mankind.

The pitfalls associated with 33, however, can take the form of martyrdom or self-sacrifice, when people put their own needs last in an effort to serve others. This can result in bitterness or fatigue.

THE NUMBER 33 AND TAROT

There is a strong correlation between Master Number 33 and the tarot card the World. This card reflects the expansive and transforming energy of 33, representing completeness, fulfillment, and spiritual enlightenment. The World encapsulates the end of a journey, when someone has integrated their experiences and reached mastery.

The World card also represents wholeness and unity, which is consistent with 33's function as a uniting force and a shining example of divine love. These two work together to encourage people to live out the values of compassion and spiritual fulfillment while they travel the path of self-awareness.

If you have 33 in any key chart positions, you can actively engage with the energy of the Master Number and the symbolism of the World card in your daily life. The best ways to incorporate the influence of 33 and the World card is by taking time to reflect on your journey and celebrate achievements. You can cultivate compassion and unity by serving humanity and practicing compassion. Lastly, you can embody spiritual development by deepening your spiritual practice and living your truth.

THE NUMBER 33 WITHIN ASTROLOGY

Master Number 33 resonates deeply with the zodiac signs Sagittarius and Pisces because both align with its expansive and compassionate qualities. The adventurous and intellectual attitude of Sagittarius perfectly reflects the idealistic and imaginative qualities of Master Number 33. Sagittarius sun signs may express 33's goals of expanding knowledge, developing spiritually, and creating a positive impact on the world.

Similarly, the loving and compassionate energy of 33 is in harmony with Pisces, the sign of empathy, intuition, and spiritual connection. The deep feeling of creative inventiveness that accompanies this Master Number's qualities of teaching, compassion, and healing are often seen in those born under the sign of Pisces.

If you have 33 in any key chart positions, you can actively harness the expansive and compassionate qualities of the Master Number in alignment with the energies of Sagittarius and Pisces. Do this by mindfully embracing expansiveness and idealism, by seeking knowledge and wisdom, and by thinking big and dreaming boldly. Overall, Sagittarius embodies the energies of adventure, optimism, and philosophical exploration, whereas Pisces represents sensitivity, intuition, and creative expression. Despite their differences, both signs share a deep connection to spirituality and a desire for growth and understanding in the world.

THE NUMBER 33 AND THE UNIVERSE

The vibration of Master Number 33 is one of wisdom, spiritual enlightenment, and selflessness. This vibration is matched by clear quartz, a gemstone prized for its purity and amplification qualities. Clear quartz also enhances mental clarity, spiritual insight, and healing abilities.

Jupiter, the planet that rules Sagittarius and is linked to development and expansion, harmonizes with the expansive energy of 33, inspiring people to realize their spiritual potential and spread positivity. Master Number 33's emphasis on enlightenment and compassion is in line with the color white, which is symbolic of purity, spirituality, and unconditional love.

Jupiter, clear quartz, and white all work in harmony to raise the frequency of Master Number 33 and enable people to live lives that are filled with altruism, kindness, and boundless love.

If you have 33 in any key chart positions, you can actively engage with the energy of the Master Number, Jupiter, clear quartz, and the color white. Because Jupiter is associated with expansion and growth, align yourself with its energy by actively seeking opportunities for personal and spiritual development. Incorporate clear quartz into your daily spiritual practices by meditating with it to enhance mental clarity or wearing it to provide healing energy throughout the day. You can enhance your practice by wearing white, surrounding yourself with the hue, or using white candles to give you a visual reminder of purity, spirituality, and divine light.

ZERO: THE INCLUSIVE NUMBER

Although 0 cannot be a Core Number, it still pops up in our lives at significant times, which means it has a place in numerology. The number 0 holds profound significance as both a starting point and a doorway to endless possibilities. In contrast to other numbers, 0 stands for the empty space, the potential from which all other numbers are generated. It contains the energies of every other number in its vibration, which is one of pure potentiality.

Fundamentally, the number 0 represents completion, wholeness, and the never-ending cycle of creation and manifestation. It represents never-ending cycles of life, death, and rebirth; the beginning and the end; and the alpha and the omega. In this way, 0 acts as a constant reminder of how everything is related to everything else and how energy is always flowing across the universe.

In terms of energy, the number 0 exudes a sense of openness, receptivity, and infinite possibility. It represents a blank canvas upon which we can paint our desires and intentions, free from the constraints of past experiences or limiting beliefs. The energy of 0 encourages us to embrace the unknown, to trust in the unfolding of life's mysteries, and to tap into the limitless reservoir of creativity and potential within ourselves.

But 0 has advantages and disadvantages just like every other number. Positively, 0 presents the chance for new beginnings, new perspectives, and unlimited growth. It challenges us to take charge of our lives, embrace change, and work with the universe to co-create the world we live in.

Negatively, the energy of 0 may occasionally be daunting or intimidating, especially for people who are resistant to change or have a fear of the unknown. It might also represent a feeling of emptiness or lack, particularly if one is not feeling connected to their inner source of strength or purpose.

CHAPTER 2

Uncovering Your Core Numbers

· · · · · · · · · · · · · · · · · · · ·

YOUR FULL NUMEROLOGICAL chart is like a bite-size map of your entire identity. It includes 12 numbers that provide insight into various aspects of an individual's personality and life. And every single element has significance; each number gives you a glimpse into a different aspect of your innermost self.

That said, your Core Numbers are . . . well, the core, central, crucial, beating-heart numbers of your chart. They're the ones that capture the essence of who you are, succinctly and directly.

Like all the numbers in your chart, your six Core Numbers are calculated using the numbers in your birth date and letters of your full name. In this chapter, we'll walk through how to find them and what they mean. Taken together, your Core Numbers paint a complex picture of you, with each one adding a different dimension to your character and journey through life. They reflect back at you your defining talents, challenges, and ultimate purpose. With them as your guide, you can navigate your life with clarity and grow into the best possible version of yourself.

LIFE PATH NUMBER

The Life Path Number, a fundamental element in numerology, is obtained from your date of birth and signifies the primary direction and purpose of your life journey. This number represents the core of who you are and the direction you are meant to take. It also makes clear the recurring themes, difficulties, opportunities, and lessons that you will likely encounter across your lifetime.

Every Life Path Number is linked to distinct attributes, traits, and inclinations that mold your character and impact your choices and experiences. A person with a Life Path Number of 1, for instance, is often driven by a desire to lead and accomplish lofty goals. A person with a Life Path Number of 7, on the other hand, may be very intuitive and have a strong analytical mind, which would drive them to pursue intellectual or spiritual endeavors.

Knowing your Life Path Number can help you become more aware of your advantages and disadvantages as well as possible avenues for personal development and fulfillment. It acts as a compass, assisting you in overcoming challenges, and making decisions that are in line with your fullest potential and real purpose in life. Taking advantage of the possibilities and lessons linked to your Life Path Number may help you become more self-aware, fulfilled, and harmonious in all facets of your life.

Calculate Your Life Path Number

STEP 1: Write out your birth date in the format MM/DD/YYYY (month/day/year). This example uses the birth date March 15, 1990.

EXAMPLE	CALCULATION
03/15/1990	

STEP 2: Calculate the sum of your birth date. Add together all the numerical values of the birth date components (month, day, and year).

EXAMPLE	CALCULATION
0 + 3 (MONTH) + 1 + 5 (DAY) + 1 + 9 + 9 + 0 (YEAR) = 28	

Continued

STEP 3: Further reduce. If the sum is a two-digit number, continue to reduce it by adding the digits together until you get a single-digit number. However, remember that if you hit 11, 22, or 33, stop right there. There is no need to add those doubled-up digits to get a single one; claim that Life Path Number as your own.

EXAMPLE	CALCULATION
2 + 8 = 10, which is further reduced to 1 + 0 = 1	

STEP 4: The single-digit number (or Master Number) obtained is your final Life Path Number.

EXAMPLE	CALCULATION
1	

THE MEANING OF EACH LIFE PATH NUMBER

LIFE PATH NUMBER 1

People with Life Path Number 1 are naturally inclined to be leaders. They forge their own paths and vigorously pursue their goals, moving with tenacity and perseverance, projecting confidence and assertiveness in both personal and professional settings. These people overcome hurdles because of their strong will and pioneering attitudes, which inspires others to do the same. People with Life Path Number 1 do well in positions where they can create, drive change, and provide visionary leadership.

LIFE PATH NUMBER 2

Life Path Number 2 is all about harmony, diplomacy, and cooperation. Individuals with this number are skilled at promoting understanding within relationships, making them natural mediators. They enjoy working in groups and reaching consensus, so they thrive in cooperative settings. They can handle disagreements with grace and tact thanks to their diplomatic personalities. Life Path Number 2s do best in positions that allow them to foster unity, communication, and feelings of belonging.

LIFE PATH NUMBER 3

Creativity, communication, and optimism are central to Life Path Number 3. These people have a natural gift for expression and enjoy engaging in creative activities and conversations. They are kind and easy to get along with, which attracts others to their lively energy. They flourish in settings that allow their expressive abilities to shine, and they frequently choose careers that require strong, clear communication. Individuals with Life Path Number 3 inspire others with their positivity and creative outlook on life.

LIFE PATH NUMBER 4

Life Path Number 4 represents stability, practicality, and hard work. People with this number have excellent organizational skills and take a methodical approach to their work, which guarantees its accuracy and dependability. Number 4 people are dependable and trustworthy because they appreciate stability in their lives. Their hard work ethic and dedication to perfection help create a structured and well-organized atmosphere in both the personal and professional realms.

LIFE PATH NUMBER 5

Life Path Number 5 embodies freedom, adaptability, and adventure. These people are known for their versatility and willingness to change. They flourish in fast-paced settings and constantly pursue challenges and new experiences. These individuals have a natural capacity to cope with the ups and downs of life, and they find excitement in the unknown. Their adventurous spirit pushes them to choose different routes, which results in a life full of learning experiences.

LIFE PATH NUMBER 6

The traits of nurturing, protection, and compassion are represented by Life Path Number 6. People with this number are responsible and empathetic, acting as rock-solid support systems for their loved ones. Their caring nature works to improve their communities as well. These individuals are motivated by love and a strong sense of responsibility; they are always ready to offer assistance and consolation to those in need. Their protective instincts lead them to create secure and peaceful surroundings, giving a feeling of safety and wellness wherever they go.

LIFE PATH NUMBER 7

Life Path Number 7 is all about perceptive, intellectual, and introspective traits. People guided by this number excel at analytical thinking and often delve into academic and spiritual endeavors. They have a capacity to solve complicated problems and unearth hidden facts, and aren't afraid of diving deep inside themselves to find purpose and insight. Their spiritual ambitions drive them to question, reflect, and seek enlightenment, leading to a life guided by wisdom and inner knowledge.

LIFE PATH NUMBER 8

Life Path Number 8 symbolizes abundance, ambition, and achievement. People with this number have a strong sense of ambition and work hard to achieve success and prosperity. They are naturally charismatic and are gifted leaders, often taking charge in both professional and personal settings. Number 8 people are determined and strong; they overcome challenges with persistence. Their dedication to achieving their goals yields outstanding results, thus solidifying their position as powerful players in the corporate world.

LIFE PATH NUMBER 9

Enlightenment and transformational humanitarianism are embodied by Life Path Number 9. People with this number are naturally charitable, dedicating their lives to helping others and improving the world. They have a deep understanding of the interconnectedness of all beings and strive to promote oneness in society. Number 9 individuals have a strong sense of empathy and compassion, and they encourage equality and social justice. Their pursuit of enlightenment drives their actions, bringing about revolutionary shifts that elevate humanity and promote a more peaceful coexistence for all.

LIFE PATH MASTER NUMBER 11

Life Path Master Number 11 represents intuition, inspiration, and spiritual qualities. People influenced by this number are attuned to their surroundings and serve as beacons of light and wisdom for others. They have a strong spiritual compass and rely on intuition to direct their decisions. People with Life Path Master Number 11 have a huge impact on the people around them, encouraging them to discover their own potential by following their goals and ambitions. Their visionary leadership and intuition create the groundwork for change, making them powerful catalysts for spiritual growth.

LIFE PATH MASTER NUMBER 22

Life Path Master Number 22 combines practical mastery with visionary ambition. Those who are guided by this number are strategic thinkers who can turn their lofty ideas into reality. They have big aspirations and are on a constant quest for perfection. People with Life Path Master Number 22 possess a rare blend of creativity and practicality, which enables them to handle difficult situations with ease. Their expertise in their careers enables them to lead with confidence, achieving their ambitious goals with calculated precision.

LIFE PATH MASTER NUMBER 33

Life Path Master Number 33 bestows the role of a caring educator, someone who applies knowledge with great influence. People with this number have a special combination of empathy and creativity that enables them to teach with compassion and understanding. They act as inspirational beacons, pointing people around them toward personal and spiritual development. Number 33s accept their responsibilities as mentors and share their creative thoughts with others, helping them reach their fullest potential. Their wise, empathetic leadership has a long-lasting effect on their communities.

Life Path Number Analysis

Record your Life Path Number: ....

1. In what ways do the traits associated to your Life Path Number align with your own experiences and goals?

    ....

    ....

    ....

    ....

2. How has the character described by your Life Path Number influenced the decisions and patterns you have made in your life thus far? Are there any prominent examples where its influence is apparent?

    ....

    ....

    ....

    ....

3. When you consider the characteristics linked to your Life Path Number, how can you use this newfound knowledge to better match your choices and actions to your true calling and potential?

    ....

    ....

    ....

    ....

BIRTH DAY NUMBER

The Birth Day Number in numerology signifies traits and tendencies that you carry throughout your life. It is derived from the day of the month on which you were born and offers insights into your personality, strengths, and challenges. This number serves as a key component in understanding your full identity and how you interact with the world around you.

The Birth Day Number reflects specific characteristics and energies associated with that particular day. For example, someone born on the first day of May will exhibit leadership qualities, independence, and a pioneering spirit. Those born on the second day of that same month might possess traits such as diplomacy, cooperation, and a desire for harmony. Each day carries its unique vibrational frequency, influencing the individual's approach to life and relationships.

Understanding the Birth Day Number provides a road map for personal growth and self-awareness, empowering you to harness your strengths and navigate obstacles more effectively. By embracing the qualities associated with your Birth Day Number, you can cultivate a deeper understanding of yourself and your unique paths in life. Ultimately, the Birth Day Number serves as a guiding light, helping you unlock your true potential and live authentically.

Calculate Your Birth Day Number

STEP 1: Extract the numerical day of your birth. This example uses the birth date March 25, 2000.

EXAMPLE	CALCULATION
25	

STEP 2: Reduce to a single digit. If the day is a double-digit number, reduce it to a single digit by adding the digits together. Keep reducing until you get a single-digit number. However, remember that if you have 11 or 22, stop right there. There is no need to add those doubled-up digits to get a single one; claim that Birth Day Number as your own.

EXAMPLE	CALCULATION
2 + 5 = 7	

STEP 3: The single-digit number (or Master Number) obtained is your final Birth Day Number in numerology.

EXAMPLE	CALCULATION
Birth Day Number is 7	

THE MEANING OF EACH BIRTH DAY NUMBER

BIRTH DAY NUMBER 1

People with the Birth Day Number 1 are often goal-oriented, independent, determined, innovative, and natural leaders. Individuals born under this number have a strong sense of leadership and an entrepreneurial spirit, and they seem to have a strong desire for achievement. They pursue their goals with passion and resilience, and their drive helps them to achieve their dreams. They flourish in settings that let them break new ground and think outside the box. Their self-reliance is fueled by their independence, which helps them to forge their own path and not be scared to stand apart from the crowd.

BIRTH DAY NUMBER 2

Individuals with the Birth Day Number 2 embody qualities of harmony, cooperation, diplomacy, intuition, and empathy. They are skilled at promoting healthy relationships and uniting their environment, making them natural peacemakers. They can handle difficult interpersonal situations with grace and tact thanks to their natural sense of diplomacy, and they frequently serve as mediators. They are intuitive, sympathetic, and deeply aware of other people's feelings, which makes them great listeners and kind friends. Their ability to work well with others allows them to flourish in teamwork settings where their wisdom helps the group achieve success.

BIRTH DAY NUMBER 3

The characteristics of inventiveness, communicativeness, optimism, friendliness, and expressiveness are radiated by those born under the Birth Day Number 3. They have a natural talent for expressing themselves creatively in various forms, including writing, performance, and art. They are excellent communicators because of their charm and friendliness; they interact with others and bring happiness everywhere they go. They confront obstacles with positivity, enthusiasm, and resiliency, inspiring people around them with their belief in possibilities. They liven up any gathering with their vibrant energy and expressiveness, making them the life of the party.

BIRTH DAY NUMBER 4

People with Birth Day Number 4 are the perfect representation of stability, practicality, diligence, loyalty, and organization. Because of their dedication to their jobs, they are the cornerstones of dependability in their social circles and places of employment. They approach projects with a practical perspective, which helps them flourish in professions that demand attention to detail. They continuously provide results thanks to their devotion and work ethic, which gains them the respect and trust of others. They value long-lasting relationships and stick by their loved ones through good times and bad. They have unparalleled organizational abilities because they do best in controlled settings where they can establish stability and order.

BIRTH DAY NUMBER 5

People with the Birth Day Number 5 have characteristics of freedom, adaptability, adventure, versatility, and change. They flourish in settings that provide them with the flexibility to experiment and create, continuously searching for new experiences. They have a natural ability to adjust, so they handle life's curveballs with grace and welcome change as a chance for development. They enthusiastically welcome challenges, and their sense of adventure drives them toward fascinating prospects. They are interested in a wide range of things, and they thrive because they love the excitement and rush of discovery.

BIRTH DAY NUMBER 6

Individuals with the Birth Day Number 6 embody qualities of compassion, protectiveness, nurturing, responsibility, and love. They are caretakers who have compassion and are always there to provide assistance. They frequently take on the position of defender for their loved ones and communities because of their unselfish character, which inspires them to stand up for people in need. Their nurturing nature leads them to establish cozy spaces where people are appreciated. They take their responsibilities seriously and work hard to keep their relationships harmonious and balanced. Their driving force is love, and they give their all to cultivating friendships and connections with others around them.

BIRTH DAY NUMBER 7

The characteristics of perceptiveness, intellectuality, analytical prowess, introspection, and spirituality are radiated by those born under the Birth Day Number 7. They frequently delve deeply into spiritual and intellectual issues. Intelligent by nature, they are curious and love to study, always trying to increase their understanding of the universe. By nature, they are introverted and often introspect to consider the big issues of life and pursue enlightenment. Because they are drawn to investigate the mystical worlds in search of significance beyond reality, spirituality is fundamental to who they are.

BIRTH DAY NUMBER 8

Birth Day Number 8 symbolizes abundance, ambition, and achievement. Due to their magnetism, they produce riches with hard work and determination, drawing abundance into their life. They are naturally ambitious, setting high standards for themselves and pursuing them with determination in an effort to achieve the highest level of success. Their accomplishments frequently propel them into leadership and authority roles, where they inspire others, using their natural abilities and resources to leave a legacy of accomplishment and influence.

BIRTH DAY NUMBER 9

Those born under the Birth Day Number 9 embody qualities of humanitarianism, transformation, enlightenment, philanthropy, and harmony. They support initiatives that advance equality and social justice because they have a strong desire to have a positive impact on the world. They go through transformative personal development and encourage others to welcome change and evolution. Their quest for knowledge and spiritual investigation is led by enlightenment. Their mentality is deeply rooted in philanthropy, as they selflessly donate their time and resources to assist people in need. Their presence unites people in a common vision of a better future, fostering harmonious relationships and social bonding.

BIRTH DAY MASTER NUMBER 11

Individuals with a Birth Day Number of 11 emanate spirituality, inspiration, influence, intuition, and sensitivity. They are born to access the invisible, led by intuition that illuminates their way. Their visionary ideas and profound wisdom inspire others, bringing about transformational change. Their quest for a closer relationship with the divine and a deeper meaning in life is evident in every part of their spirituality. They have a keen sense of the energy around them and can relate to others on a deep level, offering empathy and understanding. They leave a lasting impression on the world by their powerful presence, which inspires and motivates others around them.

BIRTH DAY MASTER NUMBER 22

Birth Day Master Number 22 represents those people with ambition, mastery, strategic insight, imaginative thinking, and practicality. They possess a unique combination of grand vision and practical know-how, capable of turning their dreams into realities. They approach everything with a strategic perspective, carefully organizing and carrying out their plans and using their resources and expertise to accomplish amazing things. Their visionary leadership inspires others to reach for greatness, as they demonstrate the power of aligning lofty goals with practical action.

(Note: There is no Birth Day Master Number 33 because there are not 33 days in the month.)

Birth Day Number Analysis

Record your Birth Day Number: ....

1. How do the traits associated with your Birth Day Number resonate with your experiences and personality? Reflect on specific instances in your life where you have noticed these qualities manifesting within yourself.

    ....

    ....

    ....

2. Consider the strengths associated with your Birth Day Number. How can you leverage these strengths to enhance your personal and professional life?

    ....

    ....

    ....

3. Conversely, how might you navigate the challenges that arise from these traits? Reflect on strategies for maximizing your strengths and overcoming any obstacles.

    ....

    ....

    ....

4. How can you use your Birth Day Number as a guiding force to lead a purposeful and meaningful life? Reflect on how your innate qualities can be directed toward achieving success and fulfillment in various areas of your life, such as career, relationships, and personal growth.

    ....

    ....

    ....

FIRST IMPRESSION NUMBER

The First Impression Number provides important information about your natural talents, traits, and possible purpose. As you might expect, it also encompasses the qualities and attributes you project upon first impression. It is taken from your full name given at birth and represents the core essence of your personality and life path. This number offers valuable information into how you are likely to handle obstacles, engage with people, and move through different phases of life.

Individuals with a strong First Impression Number often possess a magnetic presence and a natural ability to inspire and influence others around them. They could be excellent in jobs requiring creativity, leadership, or communication skills, using their innate abilities to change the world.

People who are aware of their First Impression Number are better able to completely embrace their special abilities and gifts. They may choose pathways that truly resonate with their purpose and lead to greater fulfillment, achievement, and personal progress in life by aligning with their natural strength and values.

Calculate Your First Impression Number

STEP 1: Write your full name as it appears on your birth certificate. This includes your first name, middle name(s), and last name(s). If you are married and have begun to use your spouse's last name, make this calculation using the name you had *before* marriage. If you no longer use the name on your birth certificate, use the first, middle, and last names you have chosen for yourself.

EXAMPLE	CALCULATION
TAYLOR ALISON SWIFT	

STEP 2: Assign numerical values to each letter in your name, excluding vowels. (The letter *Y* is treated as a consonant and is not counted as a vowel, regardless of its placement or function within the name.)

1	2	3	4	5	6	7	8	9
A	B	C	D	E	F	G	H	I
J	K	L	M	N	O	P	Q	R
S	T	U	V	W	X	Y	Z	

EXAMPLE	CALCULATION
TAYLOR 2 + 7 + 3 + 9 ALISON 3 + 1 + 5 SWIFT 1 + 5 + 6 + 2	

STEP 3: Calculate the value for each name, excluding vowels. For each name (first, middle, and last), add up the numerical values assigned to each consonant.

EXAMPLE	CALCULATION
First: 2 + 7 + 3 + 9 = 21	First:
Middle: 3 + 1 + 5 = 9	Middle:
Last: 1 + 5 + 6 + 2 = 14	Last:

STEP 4: Reduce each name to a single digit. If the total for any name is a double-digit number, continue to add the digits together until you have a single-digit number. For example, if the total for your first name is 25, you would add 2 + 5 to get 7.

EXAMPLE	CALCULATION
First: 21 = 2 + 1 = 3	First:
Middle: 9	Middle:
Last: 14 = 1 + 4 = 5	Last:

Continued

STEP 5: Once you have reduced each name to a single digit, add the single-digit values for your first, middle, and last names together.

EXAMPLE	CALCULATION
3 + 9 + 5 = 17	

STEP 6: Reduce the total to a single digit. If the total from step 5 is a double-digit number other than 11, 22, or 33, reduce it to a single digit by adding the digits together.

EXAMPLE	CALCULATION
17 = 1 + 7 = 8	

STEP 7: The single-digit number (or Master Number) obtained is your final First Impression Number.

EXAMPLE	CALCULATION
8	

THE MEANING OF EACH FIRST IMPRESSION NUMBER

FIRST IMPRESSION NUMBER 1

The First Impression Number 1 represents qualities of being goal-oriented, independent, determined, innovative, and a natural leader. People who have this number have a strong feeling of determination and independence. Their innovative mindset allows them to think outside the box and pioneer new paths toward success. They can think creatively and break new ground in their pursuit of achievement because of their inventive mindset. They take the lead and motivate others to follow their ideas by effectively asserting themselves in social and professional settings.

FIRST IMPRESSION NUMBER 2

Individuals who have the First Impression Number 2 radiate empathy, collaboration, intuition, harmony, and diplomacy. They have a natural ability to cultivate peaceful connections and to bring people together. They function as peacemakers and mediators in conflicts because of their diplomacy, which makes it easy for them to navigate complicated social dynamics. With an intuitive effort to sense others' feelings, they provide compassionate assistance and understanding, creating strong friendships and connections. They thrive in collaborative efforts where they create teamwork because of their cooperative attitude and intuitive insights.

FIRST IMPRESSION NUMBER 3

People who exhibit traits of originality, communicativeness, optimism, friendliness, and expressiveness are those who represent First Impression Number 3. Their humor and eloquence captivate others, making them excellent communicators and storytellers. Their artistic activities are fueled by their inventiveness, which thrives in surroundings that let them express themselves freely. They bring energy and optimism with every encounter because they possess a sense of hope. Sociable by nature, they effortlessly connect with people from many walks of life, spreading joy and fostering a sense of community.

FIRST IMPRESSION NUMBER 4

Individuals with the First Impression Number 4 embody qualities of stability, practicality, diligence, loyalty, and organization. They are renowned for their steadiness and dedication to duty, and they are known for dependability in both the personal and professional realms. They approach projects methodically and with practicality, which helps them flourish in professions that need attention to detail. They gain people's respect and trust because of their hard work, which consistently produces positive outcomes. They value relationships and keep their word; loyalty is ingrained in them. They have unparalleled organizational abilities and do best in structured settings where they can establish order and stability.

FIRST IMPRESSION NUMBER 5

Individuals who fit the First Impression Number 5 radiate traits of flexibility, adventure, change, versatility, and freedom. They are natural adventurers who thrive in settings that allow them the flexibility to experiment and innovate. They are remarkably adaptive; they embrace change as an opportunity for growth and learning, navigating life's twists and turns with ease. Because of their adaptability, they excel in a variety of endeavors and are driven by the challenge and excitement of new experiences. They bring vitality and energy to all facets of their lives, always seeking stimulation and new experiences.

FIRST IMPRESSION NUMBER 6

People who express love, responsibility, nurturing, compassion, and protectiveness are often First Impression Number 6. They are natural caretakers attuned to the needs of others and are always ready to offer support and comfort. Their compassion drives them to advocate for those in need, often protecting their loved ones and communities. Their nurturing instinct leads them to establish cozy spaces where people are appreciated and important. Their main characteristic is responsibility, as they value all relationships and support their loved ones no matter what. They radiate love, which creates strong bonds and a sense of community.

FIRST IMPRESSION NUMBER 7

Individuals with the First Impression Number 7 exude perceptiveness, intellectualism, analytical skill, introspection, and spirituality. They have an acute awareness of their surroundings and delve deeply into spiritual issues. Intellectually, they are always curious and love to study, always trying to increase their grasp of the universe. Their analytical minds deconstruct difficult ideas with ease. By nature introverted, they often withdraw into introspection to consider the big issues of life and pursue enlightenment. Because they are drawn to investigate the mystical worlds in search of significance beyond the mundane reality, spirituality is fundamental to who they are.

FIRST IMPRESSION NUMBER 8

Those who possess the attributes of abundance, ambition, achievement, authority, and success are those who represent First Impression Number 8. They command respect from others around them due to their charisma and natural sense of authority. Naturally ambitious, they establish high standards for themselves and pursue them with determination, driven by a passion for success and achievement. They can overcome hurdles and prosper in demanding situations thanks to their disciplined attitude toward life, leading to abundant opportunities and rewards. They frequently rise to positions of influence because of their strong leadership qualities and passion, having a long-lasting effect on people.

FIRST IMPRESSION NUMBER 9

Individuals with the First Impression Number 9 radiate qualities of humanitarianism, transformation, enlightenment, philanthropy, and harmony. They devote their life to humanitarian efforts because they are motivated by compassion and a desire to help people. Their transforming attitude helps them grow and encourages others to welcome change and evolution. They investigate spiritual regions in search of enlightenment, developing universal truths. They are deeply rooted in philanthropy, as they generously uplift those in need. Their presence cultivates harmonious connections, bringing diverse people together in a common goal of creating a better society.

FIRST IMPRESSION MASTER NUMBER 11

Individuals embodying the First Impression Master Number 11 radiate qualities of intuition, inspiration, spirituality, sensitivity, and influence. Their intuitive abilities are enhanced, leading them toward profound insights and revelations. They infuse unconditional love and creativity into their pursuits, inspiring others to strive for excellence through their inspirational presence. Spiritually attuned, they act as beacons, purposefully navigating others through the complexity of life. They have a lasting effect on those they encounter because they are perceptive to the energy around them, providing empathetic support and understanding.

FIRST IMPRESSION MASTER NUMBER 22

The First Impression Master Number 22 represents vision, ambition, mastery, practicality, and strategic thinking. They are visionaries, capable of having grand ideas and bringing them to life. Ambitious by nature, they set bold goals and meticulously plan their paths to success and abundance. Their practical approach ensures that their achievements will enable them to carry out their goals. With strategic insight, they navigate complexities with ease, leveraging their abilities and resources to achieve unprecedented feats.

FIRST IMPRESSION MASTER NUMBER 33

People with the First Impression Master Number 33 have the traits of a compassionate teacher, wisdom bearer, creative force, and influential presence. They have a natural capacity to inspire transformational change in others. They coach and lead others around them with compassion, fostering their development and enlightenment. They leave a lasting impression on the world by igniting creativity and fostering artistic expression. They inspire and empower others by their powerful presence, bringing about positive change, thus paving the way for a better future.

First Impression Number Analysis

Record your First Impression Number: ....

1. How do the qualities associated with your First Impression Number resonate with your experiences and interactions in daily life? Reflect on specific instances where you have noticed these traits manifesting within yourself or influencing your relationships with others.

    ....

    ....

    ....

2. Consider the strengths and potential challenges associated with your First Impression Number. How can you use these strengths to enhance your personal and professional life?

    ....

    ....

    ....

3. On the other hand, how might you navigate the challenges that may arise from these traits? Reflect on strategies for maximizing your strengths and overcoming any obstacles.

    ....

    ....

    ....

4. How can you embody the essence of your First Impression Number to create a lasting impact in the world? Reflect on how your innate qualities can be harnessed to achieve personal fulfillment and make positive contributions to your community.

    ....

    ....

    ....

INNER SOUL NUMBER

Your ultimate essence is reflected in your Inner Soul Number—sometimes referred to as the Soul Urge Number—which represents your innermost wants, challenges, and motivations. It is calculated using the numerical values that are allocated to each letter in your birth name, focusing on the vowels. Beyond your surface characteristics and public demeanor, this number is said to provide deep insight into your essence or soul.

As a spiritual fingerprint, the Inner Soul Number reveals facets of your personality that aren't always obvious. It could provide insight into your spiritual journey, emotional patterns, and natural talents. Individuals frequently find great personal meaning and direction in the traits and teachings linked to their Inner Soul Number, which usually strikes a deep chord.

The search for inner harmony, self-awareness, and personal development are frequent themes connected with Inner Soul Numbers. Understanding and embracing your inner soul number can lead to greater self-acceptance, authenticity, and alignment with your true purpose in life.

Calculate Your Inner Soul Number

STEP 1: Write your full name as it appears on your birth certificate. This includes your first name, middle name(s), and last name. If you are married and have begun to use your spouse's last name, make this calculation using the name you had *before* marriage. If you no longer use the name on your birth certificate, use the first, middle, and last names you have chosen for yourself.

EXAMPLE	CALCULATION
PATRICIA LEE SMITH	

STEP 2: Assign numerical values to each vowel. Identify all the vowels (A, E, I, O, U) in your full birth name. In numerology, each letter of the alphabet is assigned a numerical value based on its position. (The letter *Y* is treated as a consonant and is not counted as a vowel, regardless of its placement or function within the name.) Here's a common assignment for vowels:

1	5	9	6	3
A	E	I	O	U

EXAMPLE	CALCULATION
P̶A̶T̶R̶I̶C̶I̶A 1 + 9 + 9 + 1 L̶E̶E 5 + 5 S̶M̶I̶T̶H̶ 1	

STEP 3: Add together all the numerical values assigned to the vowels in your name.

EXAMPLE	CALCULATION
First: 1 + 9 + 9 + 1 = 20	First:
Middle: 5 + 5 = 10	Middle:
Last: 1	Last:

STEP 4: Add the numbers together. Then, reduce to a single digit. If the sum of the numerical values is a double-digit number other than 11, 22, or 33, continue reducing it by adding the digits together until you obtain a single-digit number.

EXAMPLE	CALCULATION
20 + 10 + 1 = 31 31 = 3 + 1 = 4	

STEP 5: The single-digit number (or Master Number) obtained is your final Inner Soul Number.

EXAMPLE	CALCULATION
4	

THE MEANING OF EACH INNER SOUL NUMBER

INNER SOUL NUMBER 1

Individuals with Inner Soul Number 1 are goal-oriented, independent, determined, and innovative. They have a natural desire to succeed and pursue their endeavors with unwavering determination. They are natural leaders who motivate others with their creative ideas and confidence. In the face of difficulties, their inner strength and determination come through, directing them toward personal development and continuous growth.

INNER SOUL NUMBER 2

People with Inner Soul Number 2 are the embodiment of harmony, collaboration, intuition, and diplomacy. They are excellent at building peaceful, understanding environments and promoting healthy interactions. They frequently mediate disputes, and their intuition helps them navigate social dynamics with kindness. Empathic by nature, they always provide assistance to people in need. Their ability to work well in groups allows them to leverage cooperation to accomplish shared goals and bring about positive change.

INNER SOUL NUMBER 3

Creativity, expressiveness, optimism, friendliness, and communicativeness are characteristics of people with Inner Soul Number 3. They have a natural ability to tell stories and are skilled at doing it with enthusiasm. Their passions are fueled by their creative energy, which inspires with many forms of self-expression. They are upbeat people who uplift others with their positive attitude toward life. Friendly and sociable, they flourish in social environments, easily bringing happiness to others. They make a lasting impact wherever they go because of their expressive characters.

INNER SOUL NUMBER 4

Inner Soul Number 4 reflects stability, practicality, diligence, loyalty, and organization. Recognized for their commitment and perseverance, these people are dependable in both personal and professional realms. They approach tasks methodically, excelling in roles that demand careful planning. They gain people's trust with their hard work, value long-term relationships, and keep their word. They have unparalleled organizational abilities and thrive in settings where they can establish order and stability.

INNER SOUL NUMBER 5

Those who possess the attributes of flexibility, adventure, freedom, variety, and change typically have Inner Soul Number 5. They welcome life as an adventure and thrive on the thrill of discovering new opportunities. They welcome change as a chance for personal development and have the innate ability to adjust to the ups and downs of life. Dynamic and adaptable, they thrive in most settings and move with ease between various responsibilities. Their passion for freedom drives them to explore uncharted territories and motivates others to seize life's endless opportunities.

INNER SOUL NUMBER 6

People who possess Inner Soul Number 6 exhibit love, responsibility, nurturing, compassion, and protectiveness. They are caretakers who are attuned to others' needs and are constantly providing support. Their compassionate nature drives them to advocate for those in need, assuming the role of protector for their loved ones and communities. Their nurturing nature leads them to establish cozy spaces where people are appreciated and loved. Highly responsible individuals, they prioritize relationships and stand by their loved ones through good and bad times.

INNER SOUL NUMBER 7

Individuals with Inner Soul Number 7 radiate intelligence, spirituality, analytical skill, and perceptiveness. They have an acute awareness of their surroundings and delve deeply into spiritual and intellectual issues. These people are very curious and love to study, seeking to expand their understanding of the universe. Their analytical minds dissect difficult ideas with ease. Their path is guided by their spiritual connection, which gives their life meaning and purpose in all areas.

INNER SOUL NUMBER 8

People who have Inner Soul Number 8 emanate success, ambition, abundance, authority, and achievement. They possess an air of confidence and assertiveness that demands respect. They are driven by a passion for success and achievement, and their disciplined approach to life enables them to overcome obstacles and thrive in challenging environments. They easily rise to positions of responsibility, and they influence people through their strong leadership qualities.

INNER SOUL NUMBER 9

People with Inner Soul Number 9 are the embodiment of compassion, enlightenment, generosity, and harmony. They devote their lives to serving humanity, and their selfless attitude helps them grow and encourages others to welcome change. They research spiritual ideology in search of enlightenment, fostering connections with universal truths. Their morale is deeply rooted in philanthropy, so they often donate to help those in need. These people are dedicated to cultivating human connections and bringing people together in a shared vision of a better world.

INNER SOUL MASTER NUMBER 11

Individuals with Inner Soul Master Number 11 reflect qualities of intuition, inspiration, spirituality, sensitivity, and influence. They have a natural sense of intuition, guiding them toward a nearly endless string of epiphanies and insights. They infuse spiritual knowledge into their pursuits, inspiring others to strive for excellence. They have a lasting effect on the people they meet because they are sensitive to the energies around them and provide empathetic support and understanding.

INNER SOUL MASTER NUMBER 22

Vision, ambition, mastery, practicality, and strategic thinking are all present in Inner Soul Master Number 22. People with this number have a visionary mindset that enables them to imagine huge concepts and bring them to life. Naturally ambitious, they plot their routes to success and set bold goals. Leveraging strategic insight, they navigate problems with ease, using their skills and resources to achieve unprecedented achievements, leaving a significant impact on the world.

INNER SOUL MASTER NUMBER 33

Individuals embodying the Inner Soul Master Number 33 are embodiments of teaching, compassion, wisdom, creativity, and influence. They lead people with loving care and understanding due to their strong sense of empathy and compassion. Their wisdom provides deep insights that stimulate transformation and growth. Their creativity flows easily because they have huge imaginations. Their influential presence leaves a positive mark on the world, empowering those around them to reach their highest potential.

Inner Soul Number Analysis

Record your Inner Soul Number: ....

1. How do the qualities associated with your Inner Soul Number resonate with your innermost desires and aspirations? Reflect on specific instances where you have noticed these traits manifesting within yourself or influencing your personal journey.

    ....

    ....

    ....

2. Consider the strengths and potential challenges associated with your Inner Soul Number. How can you leverage these strengths to enhance your personal growth and relationships?

    ....

    ....

    ....

3. Conversely, how might you navigate the challenges that arise from these traits? Reflect on strategies for maximizing your strengths and overcoming any obstacles.

    ....

    ....

    ....

4. In what ways can you align with the energy of your Inner Soul Number to lead a more fulfilling and purposeful life? Reflect on how your innate qualities can be harnessed to contribute positively to your own well-being and the well-being of others.

    ....

    ....

    ....

CHARACTER NUMBER

As you might expect, your Character Number reflects your natural traits, strengths, weaknesses, and potential as an individual. It also reveals the essence of your personality: what motivates you, what inspires you, and how you make choices. Calculated using the consonants in your full birth name, the Character Number provides important information about how you will move through life and how you'll interact with the world.

This number represents the essential qualities that mold your personality and influence your behavior and attitude. When the important aspects of your personality are exposed—including how you handle challenges, how you communicate, emotional tendencies, and the dynamics and patterns in your interactions with others—you begin to have a greater understanding of yourself. In this way, your Character Number acts as a compass, pointing out opportunities for personal development and growth, enabling you to travel through life with honesty, clarity, and confidence.

Calculate Your Character Number

STEP 1: Write your full name as it appears on your birth certificate. This includes your first name, middle name(s), and last name. If you are married and have begun to use your spouse's last name, make this calculation using the name you had *before* marriage. If you no longer use the name on your birth certificate, use the first, middle, and last names you have chosen for yourself.

EXAMPLE	CALCULATION
SERENA JAMEKA WILLIAMS	First: Middle: Last:

STEP 2: Assign numerical values to consonants.

1	2	3	4	5	6	7	8	9
A	B	C	D	E	F	G	H	I
J	K	L	M	N	O	P	Q	R
S	T	U	V	W	X	Y	Z	

Disregard vowels (*A, E, I, O, U,* and sometimes *Y*) as they are not used in calculating the character number.

Include *Y* as a vowel when:

1. It functions as a vowel sound in a word. For example, in the names *Lyn* or *Bryan*, the *Y* sounds like a vowel.
2. It is at the end of a syllable and creates a vowel sound, as in *Marty*.

Do not include *Y* as a vowel when:

1. It functions as a consonant sound at the beginning of a syllable, such as in the names *Yolanda* or *Yvette*.
2. It is used in a way that does not replace or act as a vowel. For instance, in *Taylor*, the *Y* follows a vowel but does not act as one itself.

EXAMPLE	CALCULATION
SERENA 1 + 9 + 5	First:
JAMEKA 1 + 4 + 2	Middle:
WILLIAMS 5 + 3 + 3 + 4 + 1	Last:

STEP 3: Calculate the total value of each of your names. Add up the numerical values assigned to each consonant in your name.

EXAMPLE	CALCULATION
First: 1 + 9 + 5 = 15	First:
Middle: 1 + 4 + 2 = 7	Middle:
Last: 5 + 3 + 3 + 4 + 1 = 16	Last:

STEP 4: Reduce each name's number to a single digit. Add the numbers. If the total is a double-digit number, continue adding the digits together until you have a single-digit number. Remember, if your total is 11, 22, or 33, that is your final Character Number.

EXAMPLE	CALCULATION
First: 15 = 1 + 5 = 6 Middle: 7 Last: 16 = 1 + 6 = 7 6 + 7 + 7 = 20 20 = 2 + 0 = 2	First: Middle: Last:

STEP 5: The single-digit number (or Master Number) obtained is your final Character Number.

EXAMPLE	CALCULATION
2	

THE MEANING OF EACH CHARACTER NUMBER

CHARACTER NUMBER 1

Those who have Character Number 1 will naturally be independent, innovative, goal-oriented, and determined. People with this number exhibit natural leadership qualities and strong willpower, motivated by a powerful sense of ambition. They take initiative, setting lofty goals and pursuing them with determination and focus. They can easily overcome challenges because of their assertiveness and independence, which drive their success.

CHARACTER NUMBER 2

Character Number 2 is a model of cooperation, diplomacy, intuition, harmony, and empathy. People who have this number value peaceful relationships and create nurturing environments. They work well in collaborative settings, mediating and bringing people together during conflicts. They have a keen sense of empathy and an intuitive understanding of other people's needs. Their tactful approach helps them build relationships based on mutual respect and trust, encouraging peaceful encounters and a sense of belonging.

CHARACTER NUMBER 3

The qualities of optimism, expressiveness, creativity, sociability, and communication are embodied by Character Number 3. People who have this number are very creative and expressive, so they excel in settings that encourage self-expression. They have a sociable charm and wit that captivates people, as does their command of language and storytelling skills. They bring creativity to all they do in life, including their professions, hobbies, and social relationships. Their positive view on life uplifts people around them and spreads joy wherever they go.

CHARACTER NUMBER 4

Character Number 4 has traits of stability, practicality, organization, loyalty, and diligence. People with this number are known for their analytical outlook on life. They perform best in settings that require close attention to detail. They seek stability in both their personal and professional interests, placing a high value on structure and organization. With a strong sense of accountability, they honor their words, face difficulties head-on, and emerge as pillars of stability and strength.

CHARACTER NUMBER 5

Those who have Character Number 5 value freedom, adaptability, versatility, and change. Individuals with this number view life as an adventure. They are curious and look for fresh experiences and chances to learn. They demonstrate flexibility and spontaneity, readily adjusting to changing situations and are happy to veer off the beaten path. Their ability to adapt to many situations is a result of their versatility, and their quest for freedom inspires them to overcome obstacles and follow their dreams with enthusiasm.

CHARACTER NUMBER 6

Character Number 6 is a model of compassion, protection, nurturing, responsibility, and love. People with this number are compassionate and aware of the needs of others. They are excellent at establishing welcoming, encouraging spaces where harmony and love flourish. They take on the roles of nurturers, placing a high value on family and connections. Their empathetic disposition prompts them to help and give direction to anyone who needs it. They are the epitome of unconditional love, strongly devoted to their loved ones.

CHARACTER NUMBER 7

Individuals with Character Number 7 are introspective, intellectual, perceptive, and spiritual. This number is associated with deep wisdom and a hunger for information. People with this Character Number boldly explore all facets of spirituality, placing a high value on spiritual growth. Their analytical approach and intuitive insights help them navigate the complexities of life, and their introspective nature inspires them to pursue personal development. Their wisdom inspires others, creating a lasting impression on people they meet.

CHARACTER NUMBER 8

Character Number 8 is a representation of abundance, ambition, achievement, authority, and success. People with this number are motivated by a strong desire to fulfill their dreams and succeed financially. They excel in positions of leadership and are highly ambitious in their daily lives, pursuing their goals with unyielding focus and confidence. Their natural leadership qualities enable them to face obstacles head-on, frequently ascending to positions of power and influence.

CHARACTER NUMBER 9

Character Number 9 is a personification of humanitarianism, transformation, enlightenment, philanthropy, and harmony. People who possess this number are motivated by a strong desire to help those in need. They excel in philanthropic ventures, dedicating themselves to uplifting others and making a positive impact on the world. They are strong advocates of social justice and equality who live their lives steeped in kindness and charity. Their character motivates others to join them in their mission of bringing about a more peaceful world, while their enlightened understanding helps them navigate life's challenges.

CHARACTER MASTER NUMBER 11

Spiritual enlightenment, inspiration, sensitivity, and intuition are qualities that represent Character Master Number 11. People who have this number have a heightened sense of intuition and often experience powerful revelations. They serve as an inspiration to others, encouraging them to reach their full potential. These perceptive people explore the depths of consciousness and universal truths, putting a high priority on spiritual pursuits and enlightenment. Their visionary outlook and intuitive wisdom guide them through life's challenges, while their presence inspires others to awaken to their own inner wisdom.

CHARACTER MASTER NUMBER 22

Character Master Number 22's traits include practical mastery, strategy, and ambition. This number represents those individuals who have a grand vision and the ability to make that vision come to fruition. They excel at both strategic planning and execution, and they use their command of material resources to bring their ideas to life on a large scale. Through inspiring people to join them in their mission, their visionary leadership creates a wave of collective action that can help to build a sustainable and peaceful future.

CHARACTER MASTER NUMBER 33

The qualities of compassion, wisdom, creativity, and influence are often characterized by Character Master Number 33. Those who have this number possess a strong sense of compassion and a desire to help others. They are excellent at mentoring others and leverage their innate wisdom to advance society. They place a high priority on humanitarian work and create a sense of peace by setting a compassionate example for others to follow. These individuals leave a legacy of love, compassion, and influence with their deeds and teachings.

Character Number Analysis

Record your Character Number: ....

1. How do the traits associated with your Character Number resonate with your experiences and interactions in daily life? Reflect on specific instances where you have noticed these traits manifesting within yourself or influencing your relationships with others.

    ....

    ....

    ....

2. Consider the strengths and potential challenges associated with your Character Number. How can you leverage these strengths to enhance your personal growth and relationships?

    ....

    ....

    ....

3. Conversely, how might you mitigate the challenges that arise from these traits? Reflect on strategies for maximizing your strengths and overcoming any obstacles.

    ....

    ....

    ....

4. In what ways can you align with the energy of your Character Number to lead a more fulfilling and purposeful life? Reflect on how your innate qualities can be harnessed to contribute positively to your own well-being and the well-being of others.

    ....

    ....

    ....

EXPRESSION NUMBER

The Expression Number—also known as the Destiny Number or the Name Number—helps you identify where you excel and where you struggle, giving you guidance around where to focus your energies. It provides understanding into how you express yourself and the influence you have on others. This number includes your communication style, creative expression, leadership abilities, and professional interests, among other aspects of your personality.

People may reach their greatest potential and follow a meaningful life path that truly speaks to them by connecting with the energies of their Expression Number. It offers direction on how to use their skills to discover their life purpose, find personal fulfillment, and meaningfully contribute to society. In the end, the Expression Number acts as a road map for personal growth and empowerment, enabling people to accept who they really are and lead genuine, authentic lives.

Calculate Your Expression Number

STEP 1: Write down your full name as it appears on your birth certificate. This includes your first name, middle name(s), and last name. If you are married and have begun to use your spouse's last name, make this calculation using the name you had *before* marriage. If you no longer use the name on your birth certificate, use the first, middle, and last names you have chosen for yourself.

EXAMPLE	CALCULATION
SIMONE ARIANNE BILES	First: Middle: Last:

STEP 2: Assign numerical values to each letter in your name.

1	2	3	4	5	6	7	8	9
A	B	C	D	E	F	G	H	I
J	K	L	M	N	O	P	Q	R
S	T	U	V	W	X	Y	Z	

EXAMPLE	CALCULATION
SIMONE 1 + 9 + 4 + 6 + 5 + 5	First:
ARIANNE 1 + 9 + 9 + 1 + 5 + 5 + 5	Middle:
BILES 2 + 9 + 3 + 5 + 1	Last:

STEP 3: Calculate the numerical value of each name. For each name (first, middle, and last), add up the numerical values assigned to each letter.

EXAMPLE	CALCULATION
First: 1 + 9 + 4 + 6 + 5 + 5 = 30	First:
Middle: 1 + 9 + 9 + 1 + 5 + 5 + 5 = 35	Middle:
Last: 2 + 9 + 3 + 5 + 1 = 20	Last:

STEP 4: Reduce to a single digit (or Master Number). If the total for any name is a double-digit number, continue adding the digits together until you have a single-digit number.

EXAMPLE	CALCULATION
First: 30 = 3 + 0 = 3	First:
Middle: 35 = 3 + 5 = 8	Middle:
Last: 20 = 2 + 0 = 2	Last:

STEP 5: Add the reduced values. Once you have the reduced values for each name, add them together to get the total Expression Number.

EXAMPLE	CALCULATION
3 + 8 + 2 = 13	

STEP 6: Reduce to a single digit (or Master Number). If the total is a double-digit number other than 11, 22, or 33, continue adding the digits together until you have a single-digit number.

EXAMPLE	CALCULATION
13 = 1 + 3 = 4	

STEP 7: The single-digit number obtained is your final Expression Number. If it's one of the Master Numbers (11, 22, or 33), you can also interpret it as such for additional insights into your expression and potential.

EXAMPLE	CALCULATION
4	

THE MEANING OF EACH EXPRESSION NUMBER

EXPRESSION NUMBER 1

Those people with Expression Number 1 represent independence, determination, leadership, and innovation. Individuals with this number are driven by a strong desire to achieve their goals. People with this number are exceptional leaders who pave the way and motivate others with their innovative concepts. They exhibit confidence throughout their lives, always meeting challenges head-on. Their independent attitude enables them to make a lasting impression as trailblazers and visionaries.

EXPRESSION NUMBER 2

Expression Number 2 embodies harmony, intuition, empathy, and diplomacy. People with this number thrive in group environments, emphasizing cooperation and reaching consensus. They easily resolve disputes and promote harmony between various groups. They exhibit sensitivity and empathy in their daily lives, fostering connections that thrive in such surroundings. They can negotiate conflicts with elegance and tact due to their diplomatic nature.

EXPRESSION NUMBER 3

People with Expression Number 3 embody creativity, communication, optimism, sociability, and self-expression. Individuals with this number are natural storytellers and gifted communicators. They do well in artistic pursuits and flourish in settings that allow self-expression. They bring creativity to everything in their lives, including their profession, hobbies, and social relationships. Their positive view on life uplifts people around them and spreads joy, inspiring optimism.

EXPRESSION NUMBER 4

Expression Number 4 is characterized by stability, practicality, diligence, loyalty, and organization. Individuals with this number are known for their reliability and analytical outlook on life, which enables them to do well in settings that demand attention to detail and careful planning. They seek stability in both their personal and professional lives, placing a high value on structure and organization. They gain the respect and trust of others through their hard work ethic. With a strong sense of accountability, they honor their words, face challenges head-on, and emerge as pillars of stability and dependability.

EXPRESSION NUMBER 5

Freedom, adaptability, adventure, versatility, and change are qualities that represent Expression Number 5. People who have this number are naturally adventurous and embrace change. They brim with curiosity and look for new experiences and opportunities to grow. Throughout their lives, they demonstrate flexibility and spontaneity, easily adjusting to changing situations.

EXPRESSION NUMBER 6

Expression Number 6 is a symbol of protection, compassion, nurturing, responsibility, and love. Individuals with this number value family and connections above everything else; they are born nurturers and caregivers. They are excellent at establishing encouraging spaces where harmony and love flourish. They create strong emotional ties and profound relationships by offering guidance to individuals in need throughout their lives. Their sense of duty motivates them to stick with their loved ones through good times and bad, embodying the true meaning of unconditional love.

EXPRESSION NUMBER 7

Those people with Expression Number 7 represent perceptive, intellectual, analytical, introspective, and spiritual insight. Individuals with this number possess a deep wisdom alongside a thirst for knowledge. They are excellent at introspection, and they frequently spend time alone thinking about the mysteries of life. They explore spirituality with great enthusiasm, placing a high value on enlightenment and spiritual growth. Their analytical approach and intuitive insights help them overcome challenges in life, and their introspective nature inspires them to pursue personal development.

EXPRESSION NUMBER 8

Expression Number 8 is all about abundance, ambition, achievement, authority, and success. People with this number are motivated by a strong desire to fulfill their goals and succeed financially. They are endlessly ambitious in their daily lives, pursuing their goals with unyielding focus. Their leadership skill enables them to face challenges with courage, frequently rising to positions of power. Their disciplined approach to life enables them to overcome obstacles and easily achieve their dreams.

EXPRESSION NUMBER 9

The qualities of humanitarianism, transformation, enlightenment, philanthropy, and harmony represent Expression Number 9. In their lives, these people prioritize compassion, empathy, and generosity, advocating for social justice and equality. They are excellent at philanthropic work and committed to improving society. Their humanitarian character motivates others to join them in their quest to create a more peaceful and compassionate world, while their spiritual understanding helps them navigate life's challenges.

EXPRESSION MASTER NUMBER 11

Expression Master Number 11 represents intuition, inspiration, spirituality, sensitivity, and influence. People with this powerful number are often visionaries led by profound insights. They act as rays of hope during uncertain times, inspiring others with their creative solutions and kindness. Their sensitivity enables them to empathize deeply with others' emotions, which promotes a sense of connection. They have a profound effect on those they meet, influencing them to pursue enlightenment and personal development for themselves.

EXPRESSION MASTER NUMBER 22

Expression Master Number 22 is a combination of strategy, practical mastery, and visionary ambition. People who have this number have the capacity to bring lofty ideas to reality. They are driven by ambitious goals and excel in practical endeavors, demonstrating mastery over material resources. They can easily clear complicated hurdles thanks to their strategic mindset, which also helps them transform setbacks into opportunities for progress. Through their inspiring leadership, they encourage others to join them in their cause, igniting a wave of collective action for the collective good.

EXPRESSION MASTER NUMBER 33

Expression Master Number 33 is a creative visionary, a wise influencer, and a loving teacher all rolled into one. People who have this number possess creativity and insight that they apply to life-changing projects. They act as compassionate mentors who influence others, and their powerful presence encourages peace and understanding while inspiring significant transformations. They impact countless lives with their leadership and teachings, leaving a legacy of love and knowledge in their wake.

Expression Number Analysis

Record your Expression Number: ....

1. How do the traits associated with your Expression Number resonate with your experiences and aspirations in life? Reflect on specific instances where you have noticed these traits influencing your actions, decisions, and relationships.

....

....

....

2. Consider the strengths and challenges inherent in your Expression Number. How can you leverage your strengths to maximize your potential and achieve your goals?

....

....

....

3. On the flip side, how might you navigate the challenges associated with these traits?

....

....

....

4. Reflect on the impact you wish to make in the world and how your Expression Number can guide you in fulfilling your purpose. How can you align with the energies of your Expression Number to create a meaningful and fulfilling life path?

....

....

....

Your Core Numbers in a Nutshell

Now that you've got all six of your Core Numbers calculated, how do you feel? Do they accurately reflect the version of you that you believe you present to the world? Compile them all here so you can review them as a group.

MY LIFE PATH NUMBER: ....

Summary of its meaning: ....

....

....

My notes: ....

....

MY BIRTH DAY NUMBER: ....

Summary of its meaning: ....

....

....

My notes: ....

....

MY FIRST IMPRESSION NUMBER: ....

Summary of its meaning: ....

....

....

My notes: ....

....

MY INNER SOUL NUMBER: ....

    Summary of its meaning: ....

    ....

    ....

    My notes: ....

    ....

MY CHARACTER NUMBER: ....

    Summary of its meaning: ....

    ....

    ....

    My notes: ....

    ....

MY EXPRESSION NUMBER: ....

    Summary of its meaning: ....

    ....

    ....

    My notes: ....

    ....

CHAPTER 3

Exploring Your Cycles

WHEN YOU'RE READY to push beyond your Core Numbers, there's plenty more to explore! While your Core Numbers—such as Birth Day, Life Path, and Expression—provide information about essential characteristics, your Cycle Numbers shed light on the recurrent themes and patterns that appear throughout your journey. This set of numbers includes your Personal Year, Personal Month, Personal Day, Karmic Lesson, Maturity, and Karmic Debt Numbers.

Your Cycle Numbers lead you through the cycle of life by highlighting times of development, challenges, and transformations. Every Cycle Number has a corresponding time period that influences opportunity and experiences. Numerological analysis is so much more revealing when your Cycle Numbers and Core Numbers are integrated. Without your Cycle Numbers, you're missing out on valuable perspective on your behaviors and choices within the larger story of your life's development.

Through the calculation of these numbers, you're creating a custom tool for interpreting the cycles within your own destiny and harnessing numerology as a means of empowerment and self-discovery.

PERSONAL YEAR NUMBER

Have you ever wondered what themes will shape your journey in the year to come? Your Personal Year Number holds the key. It's like a road map, streamlined from the digits of the current year into a single number. This little number packs a punch, giving insights into what's ahead—highs, lows, and the general atmosphere of the events that await you. Think of it as your trusty compass, pointing you toward opportunities and warning you of potential detours. For example, a Personal Year Number of 3 signals a time for creativity and socializing, whereas a 7 hints at introspection and spiritual growth.

Understanding this number helps you align yourself with the flow of the universe, making better decisions and taking advantage of the right moments. It's like having a wise friend whispering guidance in your ear as you navigate life's twists and turns.

Calculate Your Personal Year Number

STEP 1: Write your birth date. Start by writing the day and month of your birth date in the format MM/DD (month/day). This example uses the birth date October 15.

EXAMPLE	CALCULATION
10/15	

STEP 2: Write down the four-digit *current* year.

EXAMPLE	CALCULATION
2025	

STEP 3: Reduce your birth month to a single digit by adding the digits together.

EXAMPLE	CALCULATION
1 + 0 = 1	

STEP 4: Reduce your birth day to a single digit by adding the digits together.

EXAMPLE	CALCULATION
1 + 5 = 6	

STEP 5: Add all four digits of the current year together and reduce to a single digit.

EXAMPLE	CALCULATION
2 + 0 + 2 + 5 = 9	

STEP 6: Add the reduced birth month, birth day, and current year numbers together. Add the single-digit birth month, birth day, and current year numbers.

EXAMPLE	CALCULATION
1 + 6 + 9 = 16	

STEP 7: Reduce the total to a single digit. If the sum is a double-digit number other than 11, 22, or 33, reduce it to a single digit by adding the digits together

EXAMPLE	CALCULATION
16 = 1 + 6 = 7	

THE MEANING OF EACH PERSONAL YEAR NUMBER

PERSONAL YEAR NUMBER 1

Year Number 1 signifies new beginnings, independence, and ambition. It's your time to shine, with fresh starts and bold beginnings on the horizon. This year is all about taking the lead, embracing your independence, and forging ahead with confidence. This is a moment to seize possibilities for personal development, act decisively, and sow the seeds of future success. Challenges may arise as you navigate uncharted territory, but each hurdle is an opportunity to prove your resilience and strength, setting the stage for exciting new adventures and personal growth.

PERSONAL YEAR NUMBER 2

Partnerships, harmony, and cooperation are represented by Year Number 2. Get ready to cultivate balance and deepen connections in your life. This year emphasizes cooperation, diplomacy, and partnerships. This is the time to build connections, encourage cooperation, and look for ways to compromise in both personal and professional atmospheres. Obstacles may surface as you learn to balance your needs with those of others, but every compromise brings you closer to mutual understanding and shared success, fostering deeper bonds and meaningful relationships.

PERSONAL YEAR NUMBER 3

Welcome to a year of creativity, self-expression, and social delights. It's time to let your inner artist shine and explore new avenues of self-discovery. You may feel inspired to explore your artistic talents, pursue new hobbies, or engage in meaningful conversations. It's a time for embracing joy, spontaneity, and optimism, allowing creative endeavors to flourish. Difficulties may arise as you navigate distractions or self-doubt, but each hurdle is an opportunity to tap into your creativity and share your unique gifts with the world.

PERSONAL YEAR NUMBER 4

This year calls for stability, discipline, and hard work. It's all about laying the ground-work and making steady progress toward your goals. You might concentrate on creating strong foundations, setting realistic goals, and putting orderly routines into place. It's the season for focused work, planning, and close attention to detail in all your under-takings. Challenges may emerge as you face setbacks or delays, but each obstacle is a chance to strengthen your resolve and refine your plans, paving the way for long-term success and lasting achievements.

PERSONAL YEAR NUMBER 5

Get ready for adventure, change, and exciting new opportunities. This year is all about embracing freedom, exploring new horizons, and seizing the moment. It's a time of releasing bad habits, embracing spontaneity, and exploring new avenues. Year Number 5 emphasizes travel, discovery, and personal development with an emphasis on broad-ening horizons and valuing variety. Difficulties may arise as you navigate uncertainty or unexpected twists, but each curveball is a chance to embrace spontaneity and adaptabil-ity, leading to exhilarating experiences and personal growth.

PERSONAL YEAR NUMBER 6

Love, family, and home take center stage this year. It's a time for nurturing relation-ships, creating harmony, and finding balance in your life. You'll need to prioritize family needs, establish a feeling of community, and strike a balance between personal and professional commitments. Year Number 6 is characterized by acts of compassion, service, and family pursuits that provide emotional stability. Obstacles may surface as you juggle responsibilities or face conflicts, but each hurdle is an opportunity to deepen your bonds with loved ones and cultivate a sense of security and belonging.

PERSONAL YEAR NUMBER 7

This year is one of introspection, spiritual growth, and inner wisdom. It's time to dive deep into your inner world, seeking answers and insights that can guide you on your journey. Take advantage by spending time alone, practicing meditation, and studying spiritual concepts. Intuition, learning, and spiritual development are prioritized, which shows you a more profound comprehension of yourself and the universe. Challenges may arise as you confront your fears or face uncertainty, but each moment of solitude or reflection is a chance to connect with your higher self and uncover hidden truths, leading to profound personal transformation.

PERSONAL YEAR NUMBER 8

This year is all about abundance, success, and achievement. It's time to step into your power, take charge of your destiny, and turn your dreams into reality. You'll want to focus on material goals, financial success, and professional advancement. This is the year for calculated risks, boldness, and strategic planning. Obstacles may emerge as you navigate power dynamics or financial matters, but each challenge is an opportunity to tap into your inner strength and resourcefulness, paving the way for prosperity and fulfillment.

PERSONAL YEAR NUMBER 9

Prepare for a year of endings, closures, and new beginnings. It's time to release what no longer serves you and make way for fresh opportunities and possibilities. You could have a feeling of closure, thinking back on the past and getting ready for new beginnings. It's a year to embrace love for all people, selflessness, and charitable projects by focusing on forgiving others, letting go of the past, and helping others with their spiritual development and personal progress. Challenges may surface as you let go of the past or face uncertainty about the future, but each farewell is a chance to embrace transformation and openly welcome the next chapter of your journey.

PERSONAL YEAR MASTER NUMBER 11

This year holds the potential for spiritual enlightenment and profound insights. It's a time to embrace your intuition, tap into your inner wisdom, and trust the divine guidance that surrounds you. You could feel very sensitive, have deep insights, and feel very connected to the universe. It's a moment to embrace one's individual mission, pursue greater goals, and grow spiritually. Difficulties may arise as you navigate heightened sensitivity or spiritual awakenings, but each moment of connection with your higher self is a step toward fulfilling your soul's purpose and embracing your spiritual gifts.

PERSONAL YEAR MASTER NUMBER 22

Prepare for a year of masterful manifestation and practical wisdom. It's time to turn your dreams into reality, harnessing your power to create lasting impact and change in the world. You will feel encouraged to make bold progress toward your goals and use your resources and abilities to make a lasting impact. This is the year for strategic planning, visionary leadership, and realizing big ideas. Obstacles may emerge as you navigate the complexities of your vision or face doubts about your abilities, but each hurdle is an opportunity to tap into your potential and leave a legacy that inspires others for generations to come.

PERSONAL YEAR MASTER NUMBER 33

This year offers the opportunity for profound healing and compassionate service. It's a time to channel your innate gifts of empathy and intuition into acts of love and kindness that uplift humanity. People may feel compelled to embrace their position as spiritual teachers or healers to benefit humanity. It's a time to take care of others, create peace, and spread compassion. Challenges may arise as you confront deep-seated emotions or embrace the responsibilities of your calling, but each moment of selfless service is a chance to make a meaningful difference in the lives of others and fulfill your soul's mission.

Personal Year Number Analysis

Record your Personal Year Number: ....

1. How does the energy of this Year Number resonate with your personal goals and ambitions?

    ....

    ....

    ....

    ....

2. Reflecting on past experiences, how can you leverage the characteristics of this Year Number to seize opportunities and navigate challenges?

    ....

    ....

    ....

    ....

3. In what ways do you see the influences of this Year Number manifesting in your relationships, career, and personal growth?

    ....

    ....

    ....

    ....

PERSONAL MONTH NUMBER

Have you ever noticed how each month has its own unique feel? Your Personal Month Numbers in numerology will help you understand and leverage that uniqueness to make the most of each month of the year. These numbers are like little energy tags that give us a sneak peek into what's coming up. Derived from the number assigned to each month, these numbers reveal the general climate and personal dynamics of that period.

For example, January, symbolized by the number 1, often signals the start of a new year, buzzing with initiative, independence, and fresh beginnings. On the flip side, October, with its month number 10 (which reduces to 1), shares similar vibes of new starts and uniqueness but with an added emphasis on partnerships and cooperation. You can calculate your Personal Month Number for all 12 months of the year any time; if you want to look ahead and know what the coming months will be like, just swap out the current month number for the month you wish to explore.

Knowing each Personal Month Number helps us tune into dominant energies, guiding our intentions and behaviors accordingly. It lays the groundwork for navigating opportunities and challenges while maximizing personal growth within the natural cycles of time. By embracing the power of the month number, we raise our awareness and make well-informed decisions that align with the main themes of each month's journey.

Calculate Your Personal Month Number

STEP 1: Write the numerical value of the current month. This example uses December.

EXAMPLE	CALCULATION
12	

STEP 2: Reduce the month number to a single digit. However, if the month is November (which corresponds to the number 11), you don't need to reduce it further, as this is a Master Number and holds significant energy on its own.

EXAMPLE	CALCULATION
12 = 1 + 2 = 3	

STEP 3: Add the month number from step 2 to your own Personal Year Number for the current year, which you calculated in the previous exercise. If the sum is a two-digit number other than 11 or 22, reduce to a single digit by adding the digits together. This exercise uses the Personal Year Number 9.

EXAMPLE	CALCULATION
9 + 3 = 12 = 1 + 2 = 3	

STEP 4: The sum of your Personal Year Number and the current month's reduced number is your Personal Month Number for this month.

EXAMPLE	CALCULATION
3	

THE MEANING OF EACH PERSONAL MONTH NUMBER

PERSONAL MONTH NUMBER 1

This month is all about fresh starts and taking the lead in your life. It's a time to assert your independence, set new goals, and embrace opportunities with confidence. You will experience an upsurge in enthusiasm and energy that inspires you to take on new tasks, execute goals, and exercise your independence. Challenges may arise as you navigate uncharted territory, but each hurdle is a chance to prove your resilience and ignite your inner fire, setting the stage for exciting new beginnings and personal growth.

PERSONAL MONTH NUMBER 2

Get ready to cultivate harmony and deepen connections in your relationships. This month emphasizes cooperation, diplomacy, and partnerships. You may place a higher value on balance, seeking compromise, and fostering all relationships in both your personal and professional lives. It's an opportunity to work together, hear other's perspectives, and find balance. Obstacles may surface as you learn to balance your needs with others', but every compromise brings you closer to mutual understanding and strengthens your bonds, fostering deeper connections and meaningful collaborations.

PERSONAL MONTH NUMBER 3

Welcome to a month of creativity, self-expression, and social delights. It's time to let your inner artist shine and explore new avenues of self-discovery. This month is the moment to embrace happiness, spontaneity, and optimism so that artistic endeavors can thrive. There may be plenty of social events, cultural activities, and chances for self-discovery. Difficulties may arise as you navigate distractions or self-doubt, but each one is an opportunity to tap into your creativity and share your unique gifts with the world, spreading joy and inspiration.

PERSONAL MONTH NUMBER 4

This month calls for stability, discipline, and hard work. It's all about laying solid foundations and making steady progress toward your goals. You may concentrate on building strong foundations, organizing, and pursuing long-term goals. In all your pursuits, personal and professional, this month is the time to behave responsibly, plan ahead, and pay close attention to details. Challenges may emerge as you face setbacks or delays, but each one offers a chance to strengthen your resolve and refine your plans, paving the way for long-term success and lasting achievements.

PERSONAL MONTH NUMBER 5

Get ready for adventure, change, and exciting new opportunities. This month is all about embracing freedom, exploring new horizons, and seizing the moment. You may encounter unexpected opportunities, have a big taste for diversity, and seek new experiences. This is the month to let go of routines, embrace spontaneity, and adjust to changes. Obstacles may arise as you navigate uncertainty or unexpected twists, but each curveball is a chance to embrace spontaneity and adaptability, leading to exhilarating experiences and personal growth.

PERSONAL MONTH NUMBER 6

Love, family, and home take center stage this month. It's a time for nurturing relation-ships, creating harmony, and finding balance in your life. You could place a higher priority on building connections, establishing a sense of home, and cultivating rela-tionships. This is the month to strike a balance between personal and professional obligations and to provide unselfish dedication to those you love. Difficulties may surface as you juggle responsibilities or face conflicts, but each hurdle is an opportunity to deepen your bonds with loved ones and cultivate a sense of security and belonging.

PERSONAL MONTH NUMBER 7

Prepare for a month of introspection, spiritual growth, and inner wisdom. It's time to dive deep into your inner world, seeking answers and insights that can guide you on your journey. You may be drawn to meditation, time alone, and discovering your intuition. It's a time for introspection, investigating spiritual paths, and learning about esoteric knowledge. Conflicts may arise as you confront your fears or face uncertainty, but each moment of solitude or reflection is a chance to connect with your higher self and uncover hidden truths, leading to profound personal transformation.

PERSONAL MONTH NUMBER 8

This month is all about abundance, success, and achievement. It's time to step into your power, take charge of your destiny, and turn your dreams into reality. You should prioritize material goals, professional advancement, and financial success. This is the month for calculated risks, strategic planning, and boldness. Obstacles may emerge as you navigate power dynamics or financial matters, but each hurdle is an opportunity to tap into your inner strength and resourcefulness, paving the way for prosperity and fulfillment.

PERSONAL MONTH NUMBER 9

Prepare for a month of endings, closures, and new beginnings. It's time to release what no longer serves you and make way for fresh opportunities and possibilities. You should come to terms with their past, reflect on their experiences, and be ready for new beginnings. This is definitely a month to embrace love for all people, be charitable, and be selfless. Challenges may surface as you let go of the past or face uncertainty about the future, but each farewell is a chance to embrace transformation and welcome the next chapter of your journey with open arms.

PERSONAL MONTH MASTER NUMBER 11

This month holds the potential for spiritual enlightenment and profound insights. It's a time to embrace your intuition, tap into your inner wisdom, and trust the divine guidance that surrounds you. You will be looking for insight and inner guidance and may find yourself drawn to spiritual activities. Ideas that are inspiring may come to you with ease and result in significant personal development and transformation. Difficulties may arise as you navigate heightened sensitivity or spiritual awakenings, but each moment of connection with your higher self is a step toward fulfilling your soul's purpose and embracing your spiritual gifts.

PERSONAL MONTH MASTER NUMBER 22

Personal Month 22 is a time of responsibility and the potential to bring to fruition your wants and desires. It's known as the "Master Builder," and 22 encourages you to turn big dreams into reality by focusing on long-term goals and creating lasting foundations in your life. This month calls for dedication, discipline, and leadership, as it carries a high spiritual vibration, pushing you to align with your higher purpose while remaining grounded in your efforts. Though it may feel intense, it offers amazing opportunities for personal growth and achievement.

(Note: There is no Personal Month Master Number 33.)

Personal Month Number Analysis

Record your Personal Month Number: ....

1. How does the energetic influence of this Month Number resonate with your current experiences and challenges?

    ....

    ....

    ....

    ....

2. In what ways can you leverage the qualities associated with this Month Number to align with your goals and intentions?

    ....

    ....

    ....

    ....

3. What lessons or opportunities for growth do the energy of this Month Number offer, and how can you integrate them into your personal and professional life?

    ....

    ....

    ....

    ....

PERSONAL DAY NUMBER

Have you ever felt like each day has its own unique vibe? That's because every day of the month carries a special energy, known as its Day Number, which ranges from 1 to 9 and includes two Master Numbers. This number influences the atmosphere, opportunities, and challenges of that particular day. And when combined with your own Personal Year Number, you'll get even more insight and depth.

Knowing your Personal Day Number helps you tune into daily energies, guiding your relationships, decisions, and actions accordingly. By aligning with the dominant energies of each day, you can navigate life with more clarity, purpose, and harmony. Whether you're setting goals, making important decisions, or simply looking to make the most of your day, understanding your Personal Day Number can help you use the natural attributes of each day to actualize your desires and live more purposefully. Dive into the world of Day Numbers and start each day with insight and inspiration.

Calculate Your Personal Day Number

STEP 1: Write down the numerical value of the day of the month. Start by writing the numerical value of today's date or whichever day of the month you wish to analyze. This example uses the date of the 27th.

EXAMPLE	CALCULATION
27	

STEP 2: Reduce the number to a single digit, as needed. If the date is a double-digit number, add its digits together until you obtain a single digit.

EXAMPLE	CALCULATION
2 + 7 = 9	

STEP 3: Write down the numerical value of the month and reduce the month to a single digit. This example uses October.

EXAMPLE	CALCULATION
10 = 1 + 0 = 1	

STEP 4: Add the numbers you calculated in steps 2 and 4 to your own Personal Year Number for the current year, which you calculated in a previous exercise. Reduce a double-digit sum, other than 11 or 22, to a single digit. This example uses personal number 3.

EXAMPLE	CALCULATION
3 + 9 + 1 = 13 = 1 + 3 = 4	

STEP 5: The sum of your Personal Year Number and the current reduced day and month's number is your final Personal Day Number. You can calculate your Personal Day Number for the current day or any day of the month.

EXAMPLE	CALCULATION
4	

THE MEANING OF EACH PERSONAL DAY NUMBER

PERSONAL DAY NUMBER 1

Personal Day Number 1 is all about fresh starts and taking initiative. It's a day to assert your independence, set new goals, and tackle challenges head-on. You might feel a surge of confidence and determination, which is perfect for starting new projects. Embracing this energy will help you pave the way for exciting new beginnings and personal growth. Because Personal Day Number 1 inspires people to embrace their inner power and pursue their goals with certainty and commitment, there are many opportunities for personal growth and self-discovery.

PERSONAL DAY NUMBER 2

This day emphasizes cooperation, diplomacy, and relationships. It's ideal for fostering harmony and deepening connections with others. You may notice you are inclined to show empathy and generosity, settling disputes amicably and fostering meaningful connections. Personal Day Number 2 emphasizes the value of cooperation and mutual support, assisting people in navigating social situations with grace and compassion. With patience and understanding, you can create stronger bonds and harmonious interactions, making it a rewarding and fulfilling day.

PERSONAL DAY NUMBER 3

Creativity, self-expression, and social interactions take center stage on a Personal Day Number 3. It's a great day to share your ideas, connect with friends, and let your artistic side flourish. This day invites you to be spontaneous and optimistic, to see the beauty in life, and to share your special abilities with others. Social contacts are even more stimulating and enriching, helping to build relationships with people. By embracing your creativity and engaging with others, you can experience joy and inspiration, making today vibrant and lively.

PERSONAL DAY NUMBER 4

A Personal Day Number 4 calls for discipline, organization, and hard work. Focus on building strong foundations and tackling practical tasks and your perseverance will pay off. The energy of this day highlights the value of organization and attention to detail. You may discover that you are drawn to long-term planning and practical chores and you'll work hard to achieve your goals. Embrace structure and use this energy to make steady progress toward ensuring a productive and satisfying day.

PERSONAL DAY NUMBER 5

Expect excitement, adventure, and change on a Personal Day Number 5. It's a day to embrace freedom, explore new opportunities, and be spontaneous. You may have a sense of emancipation, embracing change and seeking new experiences. The spirit of this day invites you to embrace the unexpected, break loose from old habits, and engage in adventure and discovery. This energy encourages you to be adaptable and seize the moment, leading to exhilarating experiences and personal growth.

PERSONAL DAY NUMBER 6

Love, family, and home are the focus on a Personal Day Number 6. It's a time for nurturing relationships, creating harmony, and finding balance. The energy of this day may have you put relationships first and establish a feeling of home and belonging. There may be many acts of generosity, compassion, and kindness that create emotional fulfillment and strengthen relationships. Your caring nature can help deepen connections and promote a sense of security and belonging, making today emotionally fulfilling.

PERSONAL DAY NUMBER 7

A Personal Day Number 7 is about introspection, spiritual growth, and seeking inner wisdom. The energy of this day encourages you to dive into your inner self and investigate spiritual pursuits, leading to a greater awareness of yourself and the universe. Intellectual pursuits, intuition, and insights are emphasized as paths to enlightenment and personal development. It's a perfect day for meditation, reflection, or studying something deeply interesting. This time alone can lead to profound insights and personal transformation, making it a day of meaningful self-discovery.

PERSONAL DAY NUMBER 8

Personal Day Number 8 symbolizes success, ambition, and abundance. It's a day to focus on your career, financial matters, and long-term goals. The energy of this day encourages strategic planning, assertiveness, and taking calculated risks. Opportunities for financial investments, business ventures, and professional progress are abundant as you realize the benefits of persistence and hard effort. By tapping into your inner strength and resourcefulness, you can make significant strides toward prosperity and fulfillment, making today highly productive.

PERSONAL DAY NUMBER 9

A Personal Day Number 9 is about endings, completions, and new beginnings. You may be motivated to do good deeds and serve others, which would promote empathy and a feeling of community. The energy of this day also promotes accepting universal love and letting go of the past, which results in a deep sense of inner peace and tranquility. It's a day to let go of the past, embrace transformation, and make way for fresh opportunities. Each closure is a chance for renewal and growth, making today a powerful time for embracing change.

PERSONAL DAY MASTER NUMBER 11

Personal Day Master Number 11 holds potential for spiritual enlightenment and profound insights. It's a day to trust your intuition and connect with your higher self. You may gain deep insights and have increased sensitivity, which could point you in the direction of greater purpose. The energy of this day inspires you to follow your intuition and accept your spiritual abilities. These experiences can lead to greater understanding and fulfillment of your soul's purpose, making today deeply transformative and inspiring.

PERSONAL DAY MASTER NUMBER 22

A Personal Day Master Number 22 is about masterful manifestation and practical wisdom. It's a time to turn big dreams into reality and make a lasting impact. You will feel more confident to take on challenging projects and produce huge outcomes on a grand scale. The energy of this day encourages strategic planning, disciplined action, and making the most of one's abilities and resources to realize lofty ideas. By harnessing your inner strength and practical skills, you can achieve extraordinary results and inspire those around you, making today exceptionally powerful.

(Note: There is no Personal Day Master Number 33.)

Personal Day Number Analysis

Record your Personal Day Number: ....

1. How does the energy of your Personal Day Number resonate with your current experiences and challenges?

....

....

....

....

2. In what ways can you leverage the qualities associated with your Personal Day Number to navigate obstacles and seize opportunities?

....

....

....

....

3. What lessons or insights can you learn from the energy of your Personal Day Number, and how can you integrate them into your actions and decisions moving forward?

....

....

....

....

MATURITY NUMBER

One of the things I love about numerology is that it addresses your whole self, past, present, and future. And the future-related numbers aren't all in the unimaginable future; some give you guidance around who you'll be and how you'll change in the next few years. One such number is the Maturity Number.

The underlying themes and lessons that you're likely to experience in your later years—especially starting in your mid-30s—are revealed by your Maturity Number. This one is calculated using your birth date only and serves as a compass that points out the main areas of focus and chances for spiritual growth in later life.

Your Maturity Number also predicts the traits you will most likely take on as you age, drawing attention to your strengths, weaknesses, and potential challenges that might appear as you navigate the complexities of maturity. When relied upon for guidance, this number can inspire you to take ownership of your actions, develop knowledge, and work toward a higher level of fulfillment and self-awareness.

Calculate Your Maturity Number

STEP 1: Start by writing your full birth date in the format MM/DD/YYYY (month/day/year).

EXAMPLE	CALCULATION
09/04/1981	

STEP 2: Calculate the sum of your birth date. Add together all the digits in your birth date to obtain a total.

EXAMPLE	CALCULATION
0 + 9 + 0 + 4 + 1 + 9 + 8 + 1 = 32	

STEP 3: Reduce the sum to a single digit. If the total obtained in step 2 is a double-digit number other than 11, 22, or 33, further reduce it by adding the digits together until you obtain a single digit.

EXAMPLE	CALCULATION
32 = 3 + 2 = 5	

STEP 4: Write down your full name as it appears on your birth certificate. This includes your first name, middle name(s), and last name. If you are married and have begun to use your spouse's last name, make this calculation using the name you had *before* marriage. If you no longer use the name on your birth certificate, use the first, middle, and last names you have chosen for yourself.

EXAMPLE	CALCULATION
BEYONCÉ GISELLE KNOWLES	

STEP 5: Assign numerical values to each letter in your name.

1	2	3	4	5	6	7	8	9
A	B	C	D	E	F	G	H	I
J	K	L	M	N	O	P	Q	R
S	T	U	V	W	X	Y	Z	

EXAMPLE	CALCULATION
Beyoncé 2 + 5 + 7 + 6 + 5 + 3 + 5	First:
Giselle 7 + 9 + 1 + 5 + 3 + 3 + 5	Middle:
Knowles 2 + 5 + 6 + 5 + 3 + 5 + 1	Last:

STEP 6: Calculate the numerical value of each name. For each name (first, middle, and last), add up the numerical values assigned to each letter.

EXAMPLE	CALCULATION
First: 2 + 5 + 7 + 6 + 5 + 3 + 5 = 33	First:
Middle: 7 + 9 + 1 + 5 + 3 + 3 + 5 = 33	Middle:
Last: 2 + 5 + 6 + 5 + 3 + 5 + 1 = 27	Last:

STEP 7: Reduce to a single digit. If the total for any name is a double-digit number, continue adding the digits together until you have a single-digit number.

EXAMPLE	CALCULATION
First: 33	First:
Middle: 33	Middle:
Last: 2 + 7 = 9	Last:

STEP 8: Once you have the reduced values for each name, add them together to get the total Expression Number.

EXAMPLE	CALCULATION
3 + 3 + 3 + 3 + 2 + 7 = 21	

STEP 9: Reduce to a single digit (or Master Number). If the total is a double-digit number other than 11, 22, or 33, continue adding the digits together until you have a single-digit number.

EXAMPLE	CALCULATION
21 = 2 + 1 = 3	

STEP 10: Add the number calculated from step 3 and step 9. Reduce to a single digit (or Master Number).

EXAMPLE	CALCULATION
5 + 3 = 8	

STEP 11: The single-digit number (or Master Number) obtained in step 10 is your final Maturity Number. Reflect on the meanings associated with the reduced Maturity Number to gain insights into your evolving character, personal growth, and life path.

EXAMPLE	CALCULATION
8	

THE MEANING OF EACH MATURITY NUMBER

MATURITY NUMBER 1

The Maturity Number 1 promotes leadership and independence as you become older. You will be forced to forge your own way during this time, frequently setting an example for others. Personal development and independence turn into major themes. Later in life, you may have to deal with issues such as self-doubt and the necessity of asserting yourself. Accepting these obstacles aids in your development into a confident, trailblazing person who, with innovation and courage, inspires others.

MATURITY NUMBER 2

Maturity Number 2 becomes more influential as you age and emphasizes collaboration, relationships, and sensitivity. You'll probably discover that creating harmony and deep connections becomes crucial. Navigating disagreements and developing patience may be obstacles. Emotional intelligence is enhanced when you can mediate conflicts and assist others as you grow. Later in life, you'll flourish in settings that respect understanding and diplomacy, cementing your reputation as a reliable friend and peacemaker.

MATURITY NUMBER 3

Maturity Number 3 highlights creativity, self-expression, and joy in your later years. You will have to work on maintaining your optimism and using your artistic abilities to motivate others. This number invites you to stay lighthearted and open-minded as you age while sharing your knowledge and insights via creative pursuits. Accepting your expressive side aids in your development into a dynamic, powerful person who inspires others with their inventiveness and optimistic approach to life.

MATURITY NUMBER 4

The emphasis of Maturity Number 4 is on stability, hard work, and practicality. You'll encounter obstacles as you age that will put your self-control and organizing abilities to the test. The significance of laying strong foundations and participating in long-term projects is emphasized throughout this time. Overcoming these obstacles enables you to develop into a trustworthy and sensible person. As time goes on, your capacity to offer guidance and assistance becomes increasingly important, solidifying your position as a key figure in both personal and professional realms.

MATURITY NUMBER 5

Maturity Number 5 brings ideas of adventure, adaptability, and freedom. You'll probably face obstacles that force you to welcome change and look for new experiences. This number inspires you to embrace life's unpredictable nature and to stay adaptable and open-minded. Your capacity to handle change becomes a valuable skill as you advance. Later in life, you have a strong curiosity and resilient spirit, inspiring others to enjoy the dynamic essence of life.

MATURITY NUMBER 6

Maturity Number 6 places a strong emphasis on accountability, tenderness, and caring for others. As you get older, you can encounter difficulties that require you to help and mentor others, frequently prioritizing your family and community. This period encourages you to develop your compassionate side and take on roles that involve care and service. You can develop through these difficulties and end up being a pillar of support for others. As you become older, your caring personality continues to build solid, loving relationships, making you a beloved person in your social circles.

MATURITY NUMBER 7

The themes of the Maturity Number 7 are introspection, wisdom, and spiritual development. The hardships that come with being older motivate reflection and a quest for knowledge. The need for isolation and deciphering life's secrets characterizes this time. Overcoming these challenges enables you to develop into a perceptive and intelligent person. As you share your wisdom and spiritual insights with those who are looking for a deeper purpose in life, your insightful outlook on life eventually becomes a beacon of hope for others.

MATURITY NUMBER 8

With Maturity Number 8, the later years bring a focus on power, ambition, and material success. You may encounter difficulties that put your financial and leadership skills to the test. The significance of accomplishing goals and efficiently managing resources is emphasized during this time. Overcoming these difficulties enables you to develop into a strong, well-liked person. Later in life, your capacity to become successful and generate possibilities motivates others, solidifying your reputation as a highly influential and powerful individual.

MATURITY NUMBER 9

Maturity Number 9 emphasizes compassion, humanitarianism, and universal understanding. As you become older, you'll encounter obstacles that force you to put the greater good ahead of your own interests. You are encouraged to practice selflessness and empathy throughout this time. Through overcoming these obstacles, you will develop into a shining example of kindness and generosity. Later in life, your dedication to assisting people and changing the world for the better makes you unique.

MATURITY MASTER NUMBER 11

Maturity Number 11 is a Master Number that offers enhanced inspiration, spiritual insight, and intuition. The challenges of aging force you to develop your intuitive skills and apply them to elevate others. This time frame highlights the significance of striking a balance between your spiritual aspirations and everyday reality. By overcoming these obstacles, you may develop into a spiritual mentor and motivating leader. Later in life, you become a respected person due to your capacity to establish meaningful connections with others and impart deep insight.

MATURITY MASTER NUMBER 22

The Maturity Number 22, which is also a Master Number, places a strong emphasis on legacy-building, practicality, and mastery. Aging brings challenges that test your ability to turn grand visions into reality. This is a time to develop your potential and work on long-lasting, meaningful projects. By overcoming these obstacles, you may develop into a master builder who combines practical application with spiritual understanding. Your efforts and achievements in later years serve as a monument to your remarkable qualities, leaving a lasting legacy.

MATURITY MASTER NUMBER 33

Often referred to as the "Master Teacher," Master Number 33 represents the pinnacle of spiritual consciousness and compassion. This Maturity Number pushes you to accept your responsibility as an inspiration and guide to others as you become older. You might have to figure out how to strike a balance between the demands of daily life and your enormous capacity for service. By overcoming these obstacles, you may develop into a profound healer and mentor who transforms those around you with your wisdom, empathy, and influence.

Maturity Number Analysis

Record your Maturity Number: ....

1. How does your Maturity Number resonate with the life experiences and lessons you've encountered thus far?

   ....

   ....

   ....

   ....

2. In what ways can you leverage the qualities associated with your Maturity Number to navigate future challenges and pursue your goals as you grow older?

   ....

   ....

   ....

   ....

3. What insights or themes emerge when you reflect on the significance of your Maturity Number, and how can you integrate them into your personal growth journey moving forward?

   ....

   ....

   ....

   ....

KARMIC LESSON NUMBERS

Karmic Lesson Numbers reveal certain challenges or lessons that you must face and learn during your life. These numbers—which are frequently determined by examining the presence or absence of certain digits in your name or birth date—point to potential karmic imbalances or unsolved issues from your past lives.

Every Karmic Lesson Number relates to a specific aspect of personal development or habit that needs adjustment. These teachings are seen as karmic because they offer chances for soul expansion and spiritual advancement in the current lifetime, and they mirror patterns or inclinations that you may have carried over from past incarnations.

Karmic Lesson Numbers ultimately serve as a reminder that we are masters of our own destiny. We can build a more peaceful and harmonious future for ourselves and others by facing our past traumas and embracing growth. By recognizing and acknowledging these areas of difficulty, we can consciously work toward overcoming them and achieving greater balance and fulfillment in our lives.

It's common to have three Karmic Lesson Numbers. These numbers highlight multiple areas where growth and learning are necessary. They indicate that the individual may face challenges that require attention and resolution. If a specific number appears twice, it highlights the importance of that particular lesson. The challenges associated with this number are more pronounced and require greater focus and effort to overcome.

If your chart repeats the same few numbers, there is significant focus on the lessons associated with the present numbers, indicating intense areas for growth. Each missing number points to qualities or skills that are underdeveloped or neglected. The more missing numbers, the more comprehensive the lessons that need to be addressed. It indicates that the person might need to learn a broad range of qualities to achieve balance and fulfillment.

CALCULATE YOUR KARMIC LESSON NUMBERS

1. Write your full name as it appears on your birth certificate. This includes your first name, middle name(s), and last name. If you are married and have begun to use your spouse's last name, make this calculation using the name you had *before* marriage. If you no longer use the name on your birth certificate, use the first, middle, and last names you have chosen for yourself.

CALCULATION

2. Assign numerical values to each letter in your name.

1	2	3	4	5	6	7	8	9
A	B	C	D	E	F	G	H	I
J	K	L	M	N	O	P	Q	R
S	T	U	V	W	X	Y	Z	

CALCULATION

3. Calculate the numerical value of each name. Add the numerical values of each name to obtain a total for each name.

CALCULATION

4. Reduce each total to a single digit. If any of the totals obtained in step 3 are double-digit numbers, continue reducing them until you get a single digit. For example, the total for "John" is 20, so add 2 + 0 to get 2.

CALCULATION

5. Identify the absence or abundance of specific digits. Look for patterns in the single-digit totals obtained in step 4. Note if any digits are notably absent or significantly abundant. These digits represent the Karmic Lesson Numbers.

REFLECTION

6. Interpret the Karmic Lesson Numbers. Every Karmic Lesson Number relates to a certain challenge or lesson that you must face and overcome during this lifetime. Reflect on the meanings associated with the identified Karmic Lesson Numbers and consider how they may manifest in your life.

REFLECTION

THE MEANING OF EACH KARMIC LESSON NUMBER

NUMBER 1: Represents independence, leadership, and initiative, urging individuals to take charge of their lives and pursue their goals with confidence.

NUMBER 2: Signifies cooperation, diplomacy, and empathy, emphasizing the importance of collaboration and balance in relationships and interactions.

NUMBER 3: Embodies creativity, self-expression, and joy, inspiring individuals to explore their artistic talents and embrace spontaneity.

NUMBER 4: Symbolizes stability, organization, and diligence, guiding individuals to build solid foundations and work diligently toward their objectives.

NUMBER 5: Represents freedom, versatility, and adventure, encouraging individuals to embrace change and seek new experiences.

NUMBER 6: Reflects nurturing, responsibility, and unconditional love, highlighting the importance of family, community, and caring for others.

NUMBER 7: Signifies introspection, spirituality, and wisdom, inviting individuals to delve deep into their inner selves and seek spiritual truths.

NUMBER 8: Embodies ambition, success, and abundance, guiding individuals to pursue their aspirations and achieve financial prosperity.

NUMBER 9: Represents transformation, humanitarianism, and harmony, encouraging individuals to let go of the past by embracing change and helping others.

KARMIC DEBT NUMBERS

Karmic debt can be a hard pill to swallow. It's the idea that you may have unresolved lessons or unfinished business from previous experiences across several previous lifetimes. But sometimes we have issues, patterns, or cycles (remember, we're looking at your Cycle Numbers here!) that show up in your life and seem to have zero basis in your current experiences. Perhaps they are leftovers from past lives.

Numerology explores this idea through the Karmic Debt Numbers. These numbers are typically 13, 14, 16, and 19; they are thought to be markers of specific difficulties or obstacles that people can face in their present life as a result of choices or acts from the past. It is important to note that the purpose of Karmic Debt Numbers is not to assign blame or guilt for previous lifetimes. Rather, they function as instruments for introspection and self-awareness, shedding light on why certain patterns may have emerged in various areas of an individual's life. Karmic debt can be viewed as a chance for development and change as opposed to a punishment.

Ultimately, the idea of karmic debt in numerology serves as a guide for individuals to navigate their life paths with awareness, purpose, and empowerment.

CALCULATE YOUR KARMIC DEBT NUMBERS

1. Start by writing down your full birth date in the format MM/DD/YYYY (month/day/year). For example, if your birth date is October 3, 1989, you would write it as 10/03/1989.

CALCULATION

2. Calculate your Life Path Number. Add together all the digits in your birth date to obtain a total. In keeping with the example date above, 1 + 3 + 1 + 9 + 8 + 9 = 31. Do not reduce any double-digit numbers to a single digit.

CALCULATION

3. Identify the Karmic Debt Numbers. Look for the numbers 13, 14, 16, and 19 within your birth date's calculation. If any of these numbers appear during the calculation of your Life Path Number, then you have a karmic debt associated with that number. If your Life Path Number happens to be 1, 4, 5, or 7, it's likely that you have at least one Karmic Debt Number in there.

Let's take a look at the example : 1 + 3 + 1 + 9 + 8 + 9 = 31. In this sequence, the 1 + 9 is interpreted as 19. So this person has a Karmic Debt Number of 19 that merits investigation.

CALCULATION

4. Reflect on the significance. Once you've identified your Karmic Debt Numbers, take some time to reflect on their meanings and how they may be manifesting in your life. Consider any recurring challenges or obstacles you've faced and how they relate to the themes associated with your Karmic Debt Numbers.

REFLECTION

5. Work toward resolution. Use this awareness as an opportunity for growth and healing. Recognize any habits or behaviors that may be holding you back, and commit to working through them with intention and self-awareness. By directly confronting your karmic debts, you can begin to break free from past limitations and create a more fulfilling and harmonious life.

REFLECTION

THE MEANING OF EACH KARMIC DEBT NUMBER

NUMBER 13: Karmic Debt Number 13 is a disruption-based transition symbol that can show itself as unforeseen changes or upheavals in various aspects of life, including relationships, profession, and health. People who have this debt number may encounter circumstances that push them beyond their comfort zones and make it difficult for them to change and advance. Examples include the abrupt loss of a job that forces a professional shift, the breakup of a long-term relationship that forces introspection and personal development, or health problems that need lifestyle adjustments for overall health.

NUMBER 14: Karmic Debt Number 14 reflects on lessons learned in self-control and restraint. It frequently shows itself as issues with impulsivity or acting without moderation. People may frequently find themselves in situations where they must deal with the fallout from snap judgments or acts motivated by quick satisfaction. Examples include missed opportunities brought on by a lack of attention or discipline, financial troubles brought on by overspending, and damaged relationships caused by impulsive conduct or communication.

NUMBER 16: Karmic Debt Number 16 represents trials pertaining to personal accountability and integrity. These trials may take the form of persistent difficulties that put a person's moral compass or sense of obligation to the test. These difficulties frequently center on matters of integrity, honesty, and responsibility in both personal and professional aspects. Examples include dealing with the fallout from dishonesty or unethical activity, handling problems brought on by a lack of integrity, or addressing failures brought on by carelessness or irresponsibility.

NUMBER 19: Signifying challenges associated with selflessness and service to others, Karmic Debt Number 19 prompts individuals to overcome selfish tendencies and embrace a mindset of compassion and humanitarianism. These difficulties might entail learning to put the needs of others before one's own interests in the interest of the larger good. Examples include finding it difficult to feel fulfilled until one learns the joy of helping others, encountering difficulties in relationships because of self-centered conduct, and having setbacks in job growth because of a lack of cooperation or collaboration.

Your Cycle Numbers

Now that you have calculated all six of your Cycle Numbers, how do you feel? Do they accurately reflect your experience of the world, especially lessons or challenges that seem to repeat themselves throughout your life? Compile them all here so you can review them as a group.

MY CURRENT PERSONAL YEAR NUMBER: ....

Summary of its meaning: ....

....

....

My notes: ....

....

MY CURRENT PERSONAL MONTH NUMBER: ....

Summary of its meaning: ....

....

....

My notes: ....

....

MY CURRENT PERSONAL DAY NUMBER: ....

Summary of its meaning: ....

....

....

My notes: ....

....

MY KARMIC LESSON NUMBER: ....

    Summary of its meaning: ....

    ....

    ....

    My notes: ....

    ....

MY MATURITY NUMBER: ....

    Summary of its meaning: ....

    ....

    ....

    My notes: ....

    ....

MY KARMIC DEBT NUMBER(S): ....

    Summary of its meaning: ....

    ....

    ....

    My notes: ....

    ....

INTEGRATING YOUR NUMBERS

Using Cycle Numbers and Core Numbers together deepens your knowledge and highlights the connections between many aspects of your life on the numerological path of self-discovery. By investigating the ways in which Karmic Debt Numbers coexist with Core Numbers, you can unpack recurrent themes, obstacles, and possibilities for personal development. Through reflection and awareness, you can navigate life's twists and turns with greater wisdom and resilience, ultimately embracing your true potential and fulfilling your soul's purpose.

The following exercise will help you explore the integration of your own Core and Cycle Numbers.

Integration Reflection

1. Examine how a recent major life experience or difficulty relates to your current Personal Year Number and Core Numbers.

    ....

    ....

    ....

    ....

2. Examine the connections between the opportunities and problems brought about by influences from your Karmic Debt Number and Personal Year Numbers, and the teachings and themes of your Life Path, Expression, and Soul Urge Numbers.

    ....

    ....

    ....

    ....

3. Jot down any new insights you've had after reflecting, being sure to include any links, trends, or opportunities for improvement.

    ....

    ....

    ....

    ....

4. This practice helps you gain a better grasp of how different numerological factors interact to mold your life path.

    ....

    ....

    ....

    ....

CHAPTER 4

Decoding Your Charts

NOW YOU'RE READY to start putting the pieces together; it is time to assemble some charts and see how your various numbers interact and interweave. The process of deciphering numerology charts can open doors to understanding your inner self and life path in more detail and depth than the individual numbers alone. This chapter will take you on a journey through Concords, Arrows, Birth Path Charts, Name Charts, and a handful of others, delving deep into the field of numerological analysis. At the end, you'll understand the profound impact that numbers have on our lives, shaping our destinies, experiences, and personalities.

You will learn how each numerology chart provides unique insights into different aspects of a person. For example, your Name Chart reveals the vibrational energies and influences linked to your name, offering further perspectives on your personality and destiny. Concords clarify the compatibility of different numbers in your charts and provide guidance on relating to others. And Arrows symbolize directional indicators and potential areas of growth and transformation.

Looking at the relationships and correlations between different numbers will equip you to make better, informed decisions as you grow and change throughout your life.

BIRTH PATH CHART

Understanding your Birth Path Chart provides a more thorough understanding of your life's path than just calculating your Life Path Number. Your Birth Path Chart explores several aspects of your identity and the ways in which various components of your character interact, whereas your Life Path Number gives a broad picture of your personality and central purpose.

Exploring your Birth Path Chart helps you better comprehend the various energies and themes that impact your life. This all-encompassing perspective enables you to identify your special skills and unique talents and make good use of them. It also draws attention to possible challenges and lessons, empowering you to overcome roadblocks with resilience and insight.

In addition, your Birth Path Chart offers insight on what truly fulfills you by revealing your underlying motives and goals. This knowledge may help you make choices that are in line with your passions and fundamental beliefs, which will make your life feel far more fulfilling and meaningful. It also illuminates how others see you, which helps you become more self-aware and build stronger bonds with people.

Ultimately, working your Birth Path Chart means crafting a comprehensive road map for your personal development and fulfillment. It helps you connect your actions with who you really are by integrating different aspects of your personality and life experiences. Your Birth Path Chart's energies and themes can help you navigate life's path with more confidence, purpose, and clarity.

Calculate Your Birth Path Chart

STEP 1: Start by writing down your full birth date in the format MM/DD/YYYY (month/day/year).

EXAMPLE	CALCULATION
MARCH 25, 2000 03/25/2000	

STEP 2: Create your initial sums. Calculate the sums of your birth date month, day, and year individually. For example:

EXAMPLE	CALCULATION
Birth month: 0 + 3 = 3	Birth month:
Birth day: 25 = 2 + 5 = 7	Birth day:
Birth year: 2000 = 2 + 0 + 0 + 0 = 2	Birth year:

STEP 3: Reduce your initial sums, as needed. If any two-digit numbers remain after these initial calculations, reduce each sum to a single digit. Do this by adding the digits together until you obtain a single digit, as follows:

EXAMPLE	CALCULATION
Birth month: 12 = 1 + 2 = 3	Birth month:
Birth day: 27 = 2 + 7 = 9	Birth day:
Birth year: 22 = 2 + 2 = 4	Birth year:

STEP 4: Add the reduced sums together. Once you have reduced each component to a single digit, add the three single-digit numbers (your month, day, and year numbers) together to obtain your result.

EXAMPLE	CALCULATION
3 + 9 + 4 = 16	

STEP 5: Reduce the sum to a single digit (if necessary). If the total obtained in step 4 is a double-digit number other than 11 or 22, further reduce it by adding the digits together until you obtain a single digit.

EXAMPLE	CALCULATION
16 = 1 + 6 = 7	

STEP 6: The single-digit number (or Master Number) obtained in step 5 is your final Birth Path Number, which represents your core identity and life purpose. Reflect on the qualities associated with your Birth Path Number to gain insights into your personality, strengths, and life path.

EXAMPLE	CALCULATION
7	

THE MEANING OF EACH BIRTH PATH NUMBER

As you may have noticed by now, the numbers we study in numerology have similar meanings across applications. The number 7 is always going to have something to do with spirituality and an analytical nature; the number 4 is always going to be about strength and efficiency.

With this in mind, I've included a brief recap of the numbers and their meanings here. If you'd like to dig deeper into the meaning of your Birth Path Number, turn back to chapter 1 and review the number profiles in depth.

THE MEANING OF EACH BIRTH PATH NUMBER

NUMBER 1: Represents independence, leadership, and initiative, urging individuals to take charge of their lives and pursue their goals with confidence.

NUMBER 2: Signifies cooperation, diplomacy, and empathy, emphasizing the importance of collaboration and balance in relationships and interactions.

NUMBER 3: Embodies creativity, self-expression, and joy, inspiring individuals to explore their artistic talents and embrace spontaneity.

NUMBER 4: Symbolizes stability, organization, and diligence, guiding individuals to build solid foundations and work diligently toward their objectives.

NUMBER 5: Represents freedom, versatility, and adventure, encouraging individuals to embrace change and seek new experiences.

NUMBER 6: Reflects nurturing, responsibility, and unconditional love, highlighting the importance of family, community, and caring for others.

NUMBER 7: Signifies introspection, spirituality, and wisdom, inviting individuals to delve deep into their inner selves and seek spiritual truths.

NUMBER 8: Embodies ambition, success, and abundance, guiding individuals to pursue their aspirations and achieve financial prosperity.

NUMBER 9: Represents transformation, humanitarianism, and harmony, encouraging individuals to let go of the past by embracing change and helping others.

MASTER NUMBER 11: Symbolizes intuition, spiritual enlightenment, profound insights, and the higher self, and urges individuals to push the limitations of the human experience.

MASTER NUMBER 22: Signifies potential, productivity, creativity, drive, determination, and the need to create something that supports the common good.

MASTER NUMBER 33: Embodies harmony, unity, teaching, selflessness, and pure love, and emphasizes the importance of helping others and fostering unity.

Birth Path Number Analysis

1. How do the qualities associated with your Birth Path Number resonate with your personality and life experiences? Reflect on specific instances where you see these qualities manifesting in your life.

   ....
   ....
   ....

2. Consider any challenges you've come across that align with the themes of your Birth Path Number. How can you take advantage of your strengths and natural abilities to overcome these obstacles and succeed?

   ....
   ....
   ....

3. Reflect on the life lessons and themes suggested by your Birth Path Number. How might these insights guide you in making decisions and navigating your life path with greater clarity and purpose?

   ....
   ....
   ....

4. Explore how your Birth Path Number influences your relationships and interactions with others. Are there patterns you've noticed in your relationships that resonate with the qualities of your Birth Path Number?

   ....
   ....
   ....
   ....

INTERPRETING PATTERNS AND ANOMALIES

Numerology relies on a variety of patterns and anomalies in a chart to provide deep insights into a person's life path, personality, strengths, and weaknesses. The following will explain how to tease these out of your chart and understand their significance:

REPEAT NUMBERS: When a number occurs more than once in a chart, it highlights the energy and characteristics linked to that number. For instance, if your chart has several 4s, it suggests that you place a high value on stability, organizational skills, and dependability.

MISSING NUMBERS: On the other hand, missing numbers indicate possible imbalances in your chart. For example, if your chart does not include the number 5, it can indicate that you struggle to accept change or be flexible. To create balance, you might want to ponder the meaning of these missing numbers and incorporate the traits connected to them into your life.

MASTER NUMBERS: Master Numbers 11, 22, and 33 carry heightened vibrational frequencies and spiritual significance. They show higher states of awareness as well as the possibility of spiritual development and manifestation. Master Numbers in your chart can indicate opportunities and possible challenges for your life purpose and spiritual growth.

KARMIC NUMBERS: Karmic Numbers 13, 14, 16, and 19 are symbolic of unfinished business from previous lives, lessons learned, or obstacles faced, as we learned in chapter 3. They point out places where you might keep running into setbacks unless you recognize and deal with the underlying karmic patterns. To overcome these limitations, you should consider the meaning of these Karmic Numbers in your chart and take proactive measures for growth and healing.

By keeping a sharp eye out for these patterns and anomalies, you can navigate life's journey with greater clarity, purpose, and empowerment.

NAME CHART

Creating a Name Chart is a fabulous way to learn more about the vibrational energy and influences connected to your unique name. As you walk through this calculation, layers of information about your personality, strengths, weaknesses, and destiny will reveal themselves, giving you a greater comprehension of the hidden forces at work in your life.

In addition to calculating your chart and considering its meaning, you can investigate the effects of missing or repeated letters, which provide further levels of complexity and meaning, as well as the influence of vowel and consonant letters. Dig even deeper by comparing your Birth Path and Name Charts, a process that offers a glimpse into any potential conflicts or alignments between your inner essence (Name) and outward expression (Birth Path).

Creating a numerological Name Chart is an empowering and enlightening experience. You can gain helpful insight into your true nature and purpose by exploring the hidden meaning and importance of your name.

Calculate Your Name Chart

STEP 1: Write your full name as it appears on your birth certificate. This includes your first name, middle name(s), and last name. If you are married and have begun to use your spouse's last name, make this calculation using the name you had *before* marriage. If you no longer use the name on your birth certificate, use the first, middle, and last names you have chosen for yourself.

EXAMPLE	CALCULATION
FAE MYENNE NG	

STEP 2: Assign numerical values to each letter in your name:

1	2	3	4	5	6	7	8	9
A	B	C	D	E	F	G	H	I
J	K	L	M	N	O	P	Q	R
S	T	U	V	W	X	Y	Z	

EXAMPLE	CALCULATION
First: 6 + 1 + 5	First:
Middle: 4 + 7 + 5 + 5 + 5 + 5	Middle:
Last: 5 + 7	Last:

STEP 3: Calculate the value for each name. For each name (first, middle, and last), add up the numerical values assigned to each letter.

EXAMPLE	CALCULATION
First: 6 + 1 + 5 = 12	First:
Middle: 4 + 7 + 5 + 5 + 5 + 5 = 31	Middle:
Last: 5 + 7 = 12	Last:

STEP 4: Reduce each name to a single digit. If the total for any name is a double-digit number, continue to add the digits together until you have a single-digit number. For example, if the total for your first name is 25, add 2 + 5 to get 7.

EXAMPLE	CALCULATION
First: 12 = 1 + 2 = 3	First:
Middle: 31 = 3 + 1 = 4	Middle:
Last: 12 = 1 + 2 = 3	Last:

STEP 5: Interpret the results. The single-digit numbers obtained for each component of your name represent the vibrational energies and influences associated with that part of your name. Reflect on the qualities associated with each number and consider how they resonate with your personality, strengths, and challenges.

REFLECTION

INTERPRETING PATTERNS AND ANOMALIES

Your personality, life path, strengths, and weaknesses are woven through your Name Chart through a variety of patterns and anomalies. The following is a thorough breakdown of the different results and their significance:

REPEAT NUMBERS: When a number occurs more than once in a name chart, it highlights the energy and characteristics linked to that number. If your name includes many occurrences of the number 3, for instance, it may indicate that you place a high value on self-expression, creativity, and communication. You can understand the significance of utilizing and enhancing these qualities in your life, accepting your capacity for creativity and genuine self-expression.

MISSING NUMBERS: On the other hand, missing numbers in a Name Chart draw attention to possible imbalance or underdevelopment. If your name doesn't contain the number 5, for example, it can indicate difficulties with change, flexibility, and adventure. To attain more balance and fulfillment, you might consider the meaning of these missing numbers and incorporate the traits connected with them into your life.

MASTER NUMBERS: In a Name Chart, Master Numbers have higher vibrational frequencies and spiritual meaning (just as they do in Birth Path Charts). They stand for higher states of awareness as well as the possibility of spiritual development and manifestation. Master Numbers in your Name Chart might indicate more opportunities and difficulties pertaining to your life purpose and spiritual development. Master Numbers urge you to aspire to become a higher being of intuition, inspiration, and transformation.

KARMIC NUMBERS: In a Name Chart, Karmic Numbers represent unsolved lessons or challenges from previous experiences or lifetimes. They point out places where you might keep running into problems unless you recognize and deal with the karmic patterns. To overcome previous limitations, you might consider the meaning of these Karmic Numbers in your chart and take steps for healing and development.

Name Chart Analysis

1. How do the qualities associated with each number that makes up your full name—your first name number, middle name number, and last name number—resonate with your personality and life experiences? Reflect on specific instances where you see these qualities developing in your life.

....

....

....

....

2. Consider any patterns in your name chart, such as repeat numbers, missing numbers, or Master Numbers. How do these patterns reflect aspects of your personality and life path and how can you begin to use these numbers to your advantage?

....

....

....

....

3. Explore the connection between your name chart and your birth path chart. Are there similarities or conflicts between the energies represented in both charts? How can you integrate these insights into your self-awareness and personal and/or spiritual development journey?

....

....

....

....

CONCORDS

The harmonic alignments or compatibility between different numerical forces are referred to as Concords. Certain numbers have artistic vibrations and others have a more analytical bent. Numerologists group the numbers 1 through 9 and the Master Numbers based on these similarities, and each group is called a Concord. You can use Concords to determine if two people are compatible with each other and to find out how they might align or clash based on their personalities and life paths.

How might you use Concord analysis to tap into this wisdom for yourself?

ROMANTIC RELATIONSHIPS AND PARTNERSHIPS

Concord analysis can shed light on a partner's compatibility and the potential for harmony between both partners. Numerologists can evaluate the strengths and obstacles inherent in a relationship by examining the numerical effects found in yours and your partner's Birth Chart or Name Chart. A deep and satisfying relationship can be fostered by strong Concord between couples, which may suggest shared values, goals, and emotional resonance. On the other hand, discordant elements in your charts could indicate tense or conflicting situations that require careful attention.

SOCIAL CONNECTIONS AND FRIENDSHIPS

Concord analysis can also be used to analyze social connections and friendships, helping you better understand the dynamics of your non-romantic relationships. Through the analysis of the numerical factors found in friends' and acquaintances' names or dates of birth, you can clearly see the resonance and compatibility of these relationships. Strong harmony between friends may be a sign of understanding, support, and common interests, all of which add to the bond's sturdiness and durability.

BUSINESS PARTNERSHIPS AND COLLABORATIONS

In addition to romantic and social applications, Concord analysis is a useful tool for evaluating the likelihood of success of your business and professional partnerships and collaborations. You can learn about the strengths inherent to a collaboration by looking at the numerical impacts found in the Name Charts or Birth Days of collaborators or business partners. Strong agreement between partners may be a sign of comparable abilities, attitudes, and aspirations, which can increase productivity, creativity, and success in their ventures.

FAMILY RELATIONSHIPS

Finally, Concord analysis can help you puzzle out the dynamics and interactions inside your family. You might learn more about the strength of family ties by examining the numerical impacts found in the names or birth dates of your relatives. A family with deep-running harmony may have a caring and supporting atmosphere where members accept and value one another's differences. On the other hand, dissonant elements in family members' charts could indicate tense situations or unsolved problems that need discussion and attention.

Overall, Concord analysis provides a useful framework for contemplating the dynamics of relationships and interconnections in various areas of life. It can offer you a deeper understanding of the possibilities, challenges, and strengths present in your relationships, partnerships, and cooperative efforts, or help you decide if you want to enter into a partnership with someone new! Equipped with this comprehension, you'll be able to manage your relationships with more clarity, harmony, and mutual respect.

CONCORD ANALYSIS

Comparing the numerical effects found in several areas of two people's numerological profiles—such as their Birth Charts or Name Charts—is how you identify Concords. Here is a detailed guide to help you get started.

UNDERSTAND THE NUMEROLOGICAL INFLUENCES: Before you try to find any Concords in anyone's chart, it's important to understand the numerical influences associated with each number. As you know by now, each number carries its own vibrational energy and symbolism, which can influence personality traits, strengths, challenges, and life paths. As needed, go back and review the number profiles from chapter 1 so you are grounded in the basics.

GATHER NUMEROLOGICAL DATA: Collect the necessary numerological data for the individuals or entities you wish to analyze. This may include their full birth names, birth dates, or any other relevant numerical identifiers. I recommend starting with a single chart as a point of comparison. For example, you might use Name Charts to find Concords for yourself and a romantic partner because Name Charts reflect your inner selves. Or you might try Birth Charts for business partners to see how your actions and goals align.

ASSIGN VALUES AND CALCULATE NUMERICAL TOTALS: Use the numerology system to assign numerical values to the letters of the alphabet. Assign the following values:

1	2	3	4	5	6	7	8	9
A	B	C	D	E	F	G	H	I
J	K	L	M	N	O	P	Q	R
S	T	U	V	W	X	Y	Z	

Then calculate the numerical totals you need to create charts for each person. Refer back to previous exercises in this chapter for guidance.

COMPARE NUMERICAL TOTALS: Once you have the final numbers for each person, compare them to identify any similarities or alignments. Look for instances where the totals share common factors, such as repeating numbers or identical sums.

INTERPRET THE RESULTS: Analyze the numerical alignment between the individuals to determine if there is a Concord present. A Concord may indicate compatibility, harmony, and mutual understanding between the individuals, suggesting a strong resonance and synergy in their relationship. (More details on this shortly.)

CONSIDER CONTEXT: Consider the context of the relationship or situation when interpreting the results. Although a Concord may indicate compatibility and alignment in some cases, it's important to consider other factors such as individual personalities, communication styles, and shared goals. For example, let's say Sarah and John both love outdoor activities, forming a Concord. However, Sarah likes planned trips, whereas John prefers spontaneity. Despite their shared interest, their different planning styles could create tension. By understanding and respecting these differences, they can better enjoy their shared interest.

REFLECT ON IMPLICATIONS: Reflect on the implications of the Concord for the individuals involved. Consider how the alignment of numerical influences may impact their relationship dynamics, interactions, and mutual understanding. For example, if two business partners both have a strong numerological influence of the Number 8, indicating ambition and leadership, this Concord suggests they are aligned in their drive for success. However, this shared trait could also lead to power struggles if both want to take charge. Understanding this dynamic can help them navigate their interactions, ensuring they balance leadership roles and maintain a harmonious partnership.

UNDERSTANDING THE CONCORD GROUPINGS

If you and another person have numbers that fall within a group of Concords, chances are good you'll have a solid foundation for a lasting relationship. Let's take a look at the groups.

3, 6, 9
Inspirational, Spiritual, and Artistic

People with 3s, 6s, or 9s in their charts are easily inspired as well as capable of inspiring others as these people represent very creative and artistic types. They tend to be highly expressive and passionate, and their view of life originates from a place deep within them. This group of people includes authors, artists, healers, and educators. In addition, they relate to spiritual thinking more strongly than some of the other demographics.

This group contains the 3, 6, and 9 Life Paths as well as those born on the 3rd, 6th, 9th, 12th, 15th, 18th, 21st, 27th, and 30th of any month.

1, 5, 7
Intellectual and Technological

A search for knowledge and a desire to learn characterizes the energy of these individuals. They are the intellects, the analytical thinkers, and the deeply cerebral among us. Their response to life issues is typically less emotional and more logical. They are naturally curious and often have an insatiable appetite for learning. They rule the world of science, artificial intelligence, computers, and any profession where knowledge is the key.

This group contains the 1, 5, and 7 Life Paths as well as those born on the 1st, 5th, 7th, 10th, 14th, 16th, 19th, 23rd, 25th, or 28th of any month.

2, 4, 8
Business, Money, and Management

Unafraid of hard work and with excellent business skills, here we find career-minded, business-oriented people. They are practical, grounded, efficient, and stable. People with these Concord numbers thrive on order and efficiency. They not only build businesses but also handle operations and the management of them. Here you will find the achievers and moneymakers of the business world.

This group contains the 2, 4, and 8 Life Paths as well as those born on the 2nd, 4th, 8th, 11th, 13th, 17th, 20th, 22nd, 26th, 29th, or 31st of any month.

Again, it's worth noting that context and nuance matter in the world of Concords. People who have too much in common may actually end up clashing, and people who appear opposite on the surface may balance each other out. The best use of Concords is to evaluate if both people in a relationship have shared interests and significant overlap. If those things aren't necessary to make the relationship work, Concords won't be a truly helpful means of evaluation.

ARROWS

Arrows are symbolic markers in numerology that offer important insights into a person's life path, strengths, weaknesses, and personality traits. The patterns and configurations seen in your numerological charts—such as your Name Chart or Birth Chart—are the source of these Arrows. You can explore your own characteristics and tendencies by examining the Arrows in your various charts.

Arrows come in a variety of forms and each one has its own meaning and symbolism. The most commonly used Arrows include the Arrow of Activity, the Arrow of Compassion, the Arrow of Creativity, the Arrow of Determination, the Arrow of Intellect, and the Arrow of Frustration.

The Arrow of Intellect is among the most well-known Arrows in numerology. It is identified by the presence of the numbers 3, 6, and 9 in a person's chart in a diagonal configuration. This creates an Arrow of Intellect. As you might've guessed, the Arrow of Intellect appears in charts of people who value academic endeavors, critical thinking, and effective communication. This arrow is typically associated with extremely intellectual, inquisitive, and articulate people who have a natural capacity to express themselves and share their thoughts.

The Arrow of Frustration shows up when a chart has two or more 1s, 4s, or 7s without any 2s, 5s, or 8s to balance them out. This Arrow alludes to difficulties and roadblocks in the areas of practicality, spiritual development, and self-expression. People who have this Arrow may feel stressed and frustrated in certain areas of their lives, but they can overcome these obstacles and find more fulfillment if they identify and deal with these blockers.

When a person's chart contains two or more 8s without any 1s or 3s to balance them out, the result is an Arrow of Determination. This Arrow denotes a strong sense of willpower, ambition, and tremendous capacity for leadership. People who have this Arrow are frequently motivated by a desire to succeed and have a positive influence on the world. They are resilient, resourceful, and determined to overcome any obstacles that stand in their way.

The Arrow of Creativity is formed when there are three or more 3s in a person's chart, with no 6s to balance them out. The Arrow of Creativity indicates a strong focus on emotional sensitivity, creativity, and artistic expression. People with this Arrow are frequently expressive and intuitive, and they have a natural aptitude for creative pursuits such as acting, writing, painting, or music. To fully realize their creative potential and see their ideas through to completion, they might also need to strike a balance between their creative impulses and discipline.

The Arrow of Compassion is formed when there are two or more 9s in a person's chart, with no 1s or 4s to balance them out. This Arrow represents a strong feeling of empathy, humanitarianism, and compassion. People with this arrow are frequently driven by a desire to change the world and assist others. They have kindness, generosity, and a strong commitment to meeting the needs of others.

Lastly, when a person's chart has two or more 5s without any 1s or 4s to balance them out, the Arrow of Activity is created. This Arrow suggests a strong desire for independence, exploration, and diversity. People who have this arrow are frequently independent, spontaneous, and adventurous individuals who like taking on new challenges and experiences. They flourish in dynamic settings that allow them to explore new ideas and pursue their passions.

The Arrows offer directions on how to make the most of your special abilities and move through life with fulfillment, clarity, and purpose. Identifying your Arrows can provide invaluable direction and assistance on your journey to self-discovery and personal development, regardless of whether you're facing challenges or seeking opportunities.

Find Your Arrows

In an Arrow chart, the numbers typically represent key aspects from your numerology profile, such as your birth date, name, and karmic influences. The numbers should be placed in specific positions based on the chart's design and numerological guidelines, not randomly. For example, in a birth chart, numbers from your date of birth are placed in a specific sequence, reflecting certain life paths or traits. It's important to follow the correct order as outlined by the numerology method you're using, as filling in numbers incorrectly could skew the analysis.

The correct order and position for filling in an Arrow chart in numerology depends on the specific type of chart you're using. Typically, this would be based on your birth date and name, arranged in a 3x3 grid.

Arrows are formed when there are three consecutive numbers in a row, column, or diagonal (e.g., 1, 2, 3 or 4, 5, 6). These represent specific traits or patterns in your life.

Make sure each number from your birth date is placed in its corresponding position according to this method. There's no mixing of numbers—stick to the chart's structure to maintain accuracy in your analysis.

STEP 1: Create your birth date summary. Break down your birth date into individual digits. For example, if your birth date is July 4, 1990 (07/04/1990), it becomes 0, 7, 0, 4, 1, 9, 9, 0. Place these eight digits in the 3x3 grid from left to right, top to bottom , leaving the last square (bottom right) empty.

	EXAMPLE			CALCULATION		
Top row: 1st to 3rd digits	0	7	0			
Middle row: 4th to 6th digits	4	1	9			
Bottom row: 7th and 8th digits	9	0				

STEP 2: Create your name summary. Using the reduced numbers from your first, middle, and last names (as calculated on page 174), begin filling the squares in your name chart from left to right, top to bottom. Repeat the numbers in order until all squares are filled.

CALCULATION		

STEP 3: Identify Arrows in your birth date chart, using the examples on pages 188–89. Once you have calculated the numerical totals for your chart, look for patterns and configurations that indicate the presence of Arrows. What arrows do you see?

ARROWS PRESENT	ARROW MEANINGS

STEP 4: Identify Arrows in your name summary, using the examples on pages 188–89. Once you have calculated the numerical totals for your chart, look for patterns and configurations that indicate the presence of Arrows. What arrows do you see?

ARROWS PRESENT	ARROW MEANINGS

ARROW EXAMPLES

Here are a few sample charts and details on the Arrows they contain. Each row of numbers is a different chart. The first row might be the sample person's Name Chart, second row their Birth Chart, and third row their Karmic Debt numbers. The bold numbers show where an Arrow is present.

ARROW OF INTELLECT

The Arrow of Intellect is formed specifically by the presence of the numbers 3, 6, and 9 in a person's chart. These numbers are considered to create a diagonal line in the numerological grid, symbolizing a strong emphasis on intellectual pursuits, analytical thinking, and communication skills.

    If the numbers 3, 6, and 9 appear diagonally in a person's chart, it indicates the presence of the Arrow of Intellect.

3	4	5
2	**6**	7
1	8	**9**

ARROW OF DETERMINATION

The Arrow of Determination is formed when the numbers 1, 5, and 9 appear diagonally in a person's chart. It represents determination, drive, and the ability to overcome obstacles. People with this Arrow are frequently motivated by a desire to succeed and have a positive influence on the world. They are resilient, resourceful, and determined to overcome any obstacles that stand in their way.

    If the numbers 1, 5, and 9 appear diagonally in a person's chart, it indicates the presence of the Arrow of Determination.

1	4	7
2	**5**	8
3	6	**9**

ARROW OF COMPASSION

The Arrow of Compassion is formed when the numbers 2, 5, and 8 appear diagonally in a person's chart. It represents a strong feeling of empathy, humanitarianism, and compassion. People with this arrow are frequently driven by a desire to change the world and assist others. They exhibit kindness, generosity, and a strong commitment to meeting the needs of others.

If the numbers 2, 5, and 8 appear diagonally in a person's chart, it indicates the presence of the Arrow of Compassion.

1	4	**8**
3	**5**	7
2	6	9

ARROW OF LEADERSHIP

The Arrow of Leadership is formed when the numbers 3, 5, and 7 appear diagonally in a person's chart. It represents natural leadership abilities, a strong sense of responsibility, and the capacity to inspire and guide others. People with this arrow are often driven by a desire to lead and make a meaningful impact. They possess confidence, decisiveness, and the ability to motivate those around them.

If the numbers 3, 5, and 7 appear diagonally in a person's chart, it indicates the presence of the Arrow of Leadership.

1	4	**7**
2	**5**	8
3	6	9

ARROW OF ACTIVITY

The Arrow of Activity is formed when there are three or more 1s or 9s horizontally, vertically, or diagonally in a numerology chart. It signifies a dynamic, energetic nature and a tendency toward action and initiative.

If the numbers 1 or 9 appear consecutively horizontally, vertically, or diagonally, it indicates the presence of the Arrow of Activity.

1	2	**9**
4	5	**9**
7	8	**9**

ARROW OF CREATIVITY

The Arrow of Creativity is formed when there are three or more 3s or 6s horizontally, vertically, or diagonally in a numerology chart. It symbolizes strong creative skills, artistic talent, and self-expression.

If the numbers 3 or 6 appear consecutively horizontally, vertically, or diagonally, it indicates the presence of the Arrow of Creativity.

3	2	**6**
4	3	**6**
7	8	**6**

Arrow Analysis

1. How do you resonate with the qualities associated with the Arrow(s) you discovered?

   ....

   ....

   ....

   ....

2. Reflect on the characteristics and traits linked to the arrows you identified. Consider how these resonate with your life experiences, personality, and behaviors.

   ....

   ....

   ....

   ....

3. In what areas of your life do you notice the influence of the Arrow(s)?

   ....

   ....

   ....

   ....

4. Examine the areas of your life where you see the effects of the Arrow of Creativity or the Arrow of Activity. Think about your relationships, creative projects, hobbies, and career goals.

   ....

   ....

   ....

   ....

5. How might you leverage the insights from the Arrows to enhance your strengths and navigate challenges?

....

....

....

....

....

6. What actions or changes might you consider integrating into your life based on the insights from the Arrows?

....

....

....

....

....

7. Think about potential actions or adjustments you could make in alignment with the insights gained from the Arrows. Explore new paths for personal growth, creative expression, or pursuing activities that bring you fulfillment and joy.

....

....

....

....

....

CHAPTER 5

Sharing the Art of Numerology

....

HAVING EXPLORED YOUR own numbers and charts in depth, you may be eager to share your knowledge with others in your life. This is fantastic! Numerology is a practice that can encourage and enlighten anyone who takes an interest in it, and doing a numerology reading for others can be a real joy. However, before you start making calculations for friends and family, you should take a moment to consider some best practices.

Reading someone's numerology requires more than knowledge of numerology's basic concepts. You need to approach the reading with sensitivity, empathy, and a sincere desire to uplift and empower the individual. Building a foundation of mutual respect and trust is crucial while giving readings to ensure the recipient feels secure and safe the whole time.

HOW TO PERFORM A READING

When it comes to performing the reading itself, be sure to set the tone by going over the fundamentals of numerology first. This will help the person prepare for what's to come and can prompt them to ask any initial questions. Next, have the person provide their full name and date of birth so you can create their numerology charts. (This can be done prior to the reading if you prefer to run the calculations before they arrive.) If you're just getting started as a reader, stick to the Core Numbers; they'll give both you and the person for whom you are reading a solid foundation without getting too complex.

Once you have calculated the numbers you need, start the reading by providing broad information about the person's life path, personality, and any challenges they're facing. Customize the content to address their specific interests or concerns, and check in frequently to answer any questions that pop up. Be kind and refrain from making any judgments; instead, concentrate on giving the person the tools they need to make wise choices and confidently follow their own path.

Intuition plays a significant role in interpreting the numerological insights and connecting with the individual on a deeper level. Trust your instincts and let the information come to you organically, realizing that practice will make you more comfortable and confident while giving readings. Throughout the process, encourage the person to express their views and feelings to create a cooperative and encouraging environment. The ultimate objective of the numerology reading is to empower the individual and provide direction, clarity, and support while they travel the path of self-discovery and personal development. This happens best when you are open to collaborating with the person for whom you are reading.

 ## COMMUNICATE CLEARLY

It's critical to have an honest discussion about your numerology practice with friends or clients *before* doing a reading. Describe your knowledge of numerology, your level of proficiency with it, and your methodology for readings. Let them know that numerology is a tool for self-awareness and personal development rather than a method for precisely forecasting their future, even if it can provide insightful information.

TALK ABOUT THEIR EXPECTATIONS AND GOALS: Before you dig in, ask the person about their goals for the numerology reading. Are they looking for clarity in certain areas of their life, such as relationships, their career, or their personal growth? You can tailor the reading to their requirements and give them advice that is meaningful and relevant to them, but only if you are aware of their expectations.

EMPHASIZE EMPOWERMENT: Remind the person that numerology readings are not set-in-stone future predictions; rather, they are meant to give a person the knowledge and confidence they need to make wise decisions and face life's challenges head-on. Encourage them to study the results of their reading with an open mind and a willingness to explore new perspectives and insights about themselves.

CREATE A SAFE SPACE: Make sure the numerology reading takes place in a calm, private, and distraction-free setting. Tell the person that the reading will be a judgment-free experience where they can freely express their ideas, feelings, and worries. Encourage them to relax and be themselves.

RESPECT PRIVACY AND CONFIDENTIALITY: Emphasize the value of maintaining privacy and reassure the person that both their personal data and the specifics of the reading will be kept completely confidential. Respect their boundaries and only discuss information that they are comfortable sharing.

ENCOURAGE PARTICIPATION: Ask questions, express ideas and views, and provide feedback to help the person take an active part in the reading. Urge them to follow their intuition and investigate how numerology's insights align with their personal experiences and observations.

EMPHASIZE POSITIVITY AND EMPATHY: Approach the numerology reading with a positive outlook and empathy, highlighting the person's assets, skills, and opportunities for growth. As they investigate various aspects of their numerological profile, provide them with support and encouragement and assist them in identifying areas in which they may grow and improve, but don't dwell on the negative.

PROVIDE USEFUL ADVICE: As you work through the numerology reading, provide useful advice and actionable steps so it feels concrete and helpful. Assist the person in determining which aspects of their life they should focus on to reach their goals and realize their full potential.

FOLLOW UP AND OFFER SUPPORT: After the numerology reading, ask how the person is feeling and inquire about any additional worries or concerns. If you feel comfortable, offer to be a resource to them as they put their new knowledge to good use. Continue to encourage and support them as they pursue their path of self-discovery and personal growth.

RESPECT BOUNDARIES AND LIMITS: Finally, acknowledge and honor each person's limits and boundaries. Respect their feelings and don't push them beyond their comfort zone if they indicate any reluctance or discomfort during any parts of the reading.

Respectful numerology reading takes a little bit of work and forethought, but the payoff is well worth it. By establishing a secure and encouraging environment for introspection, empowerment, and self-discovery, you'll help your friends and family members embrace this experience fully. And If you provide insightful advice and encouragement that aid the person on their road to personal development and fulfillment, they'll be so grateful. Approach all readings with understanding, compassion, and a genuine desire to help for the best experience.

 ## THE RIGHTS OF BEING READ

Reading another person's numerology chart requires access to personal information and insights that may be delicate or confidential, which means that consent is essential. Never run or read someone else's chart without their knowledge, even if you happen to have access to their birth date and full name. Always get express consent before beginning a reading, and be sure to clarify the purpose and possible results of the session. Let them know that they can refuse or withdraw their consent at any moment, without any repercussions or judgments.

Asking for permission should be done in a transparent and compassionate manner, with the focus being on the person's comfort and welfare. If they agree to a reading, give them guarantees of privacy and reassurance that the information about them will be kept secret and safe. Never divulge specifics about the reading to others without the person's express consent.

Respecting secrecy and consent can help you provide a secure space where people may learn about numerology and pursue their personal development and self-discovery journeys.

IN ROMANTIC RELATIONSHIPS

Numbers can help us comprehend the dynamics of relationships, particularly romantic ones. As you learned in the previous chapter when we explored Concords, each person has a distinct numerical blueprint that influences their social compatibility, personality traits, and communication styles. Analyzing each partner's numerical characteristics can provide couples with insightful knowledge that can deepen and improve their romantic relationship.

Because every number has a unique vibrational energy and meaning that influences our wants, desires, and behaviors in relationships, every number has some natural compatibilities. People who have a Life Path Number of 1, for example, are usually assertive, ambitious, and independent. They may look for a spouse who values their independence and shares their desire to succeed. Conversely, people with a Life Path Number of 2 place a higher priority on relationships based on empathy and mutual understanding, and they value harmony, cooperation, and emotional connection. They'll seek out a partner who shares those values.

Through the examination of numerological compatibility, couples may pinpoint areas of mutual benefit and possible conflict, allowing them to take proactive measures to resolve issues and cultivate a stronger and more satisfying relationship.

Essentially, numerology is an effective tool for supporting love and harmony in romantic relationships, understanding interpersonal dynamics, and increasing self-awareness. Couples who embrace the wisdom of numbers may go on a life-changing path of growth, fulfillment, and self-discovery that will strengthen their relationship and give it more clarity and authenticity.

There are many ways to analyze your own numerological chart in conjunction with a partner's, but the shortcut to checking compatibility is to compare your Life Path Numbers. So let's see what you can expect from a partner based on their Life Path Number!

UNDERSTANDING THE LIFE PATH NUMBERS OF ROMANTIC PARTNERS

A PARTNER WITH LIFE PATH NUMBER 1

A significant other with a Life Path Number of 1 is probably independent, goal-oriented, and determined. They take pleasure in taking the lead in relationships and flourish in leadership situations. To support their growth, you must respect their need for freedom and independence within the relationship. Acknowledge their achievements and aspirations while also maintaining your own sense of individuality. Work together on shared goals and projects while appreciating their determination and strength of character.

A PARTNER WITH LIFE PATH NUMBER 2

A partner with Life Path Number 2 values harmony, cooperation, and a sense of empathy. They seek nurturing relationships and are perceptive of the needs of others. Encourage open communication with them and let them know how much you value their kind and caring nature. Provide a peaceful, supporting atmosphere where they feel appreciated and understood. Respect their need for empathy and diplomacy and encourage cooperation and compromise. Acts of kindness and genuine affection can develop a strong emotional connection with a 2 partner.

A PARTNER WITH LIFE PATH NUMBER 3

A companion who has Life Path Number 3 is creative, expressive, and sociable. They take pleasure in bringing joy into the partnership, sharing ideas, and discovering new experiences together. To support a Number 3, welcome spontaneity and encourage their self-expression. Take part in artistic activities with them and acknowledge their unique abilities and passions. Do your best to adopt a joyful, carefree attitude that is full of positivity and laughter. Give them room to explore and encourage their vibrant personality to shine.

A PARTNER WITH LIFE PATH NUMBER 4

A partner impacted by the Number 4 is all about steadiness, loyalty, and practicality. In their relationships, they place a high value on order and structure because they want to build stability and lasting commitment. Be dependable and consistent in your words and activities to back them up. Acknowledge their need for routine and establish a strong foundation based on respect and trust. Collaborate to establish goals and plans for the future while respecting their dedication to responsibility and diligence.

A PARTNER WITH LIFE PATH NUMBER 5

A mate with Life Path Number 5 is adventurous, versatile, and adaptable. They thrive in relationships that are exciting, adaptable, and free-flowing. Do your best to embrace spontaneity and adapt to new experiences to support them. Give them the room they need for personal development and respect their need for independence. Maintain an atmosphere of enthusiasm and curiosity in your relationship by being open and flexible with your communication. Accept change with joy and celebrate with one another on your adventures and new discoveries.

A PARTNER WITH LIFE PATH NUMBER 6

A partner with Number 6 as their Life Path Number is compassionate, nurturing and protective. In partnerships, they place a high value on creating harmony, frequently taking on caregiver responsibilities. To support them, thank them for being kind and loving as a partner. Work together to complete household chores and family obligations, appreciating their dedication to establishing a secure and loving home. Establish an atmosphere of mutual respect and open communication to create a strong emotional bond based on empathy, love, and trust.

A PARTNER WITH LIFE PATH NUMBER 7

A companion influenced by Life Path Number 7 is perceptive, spiritually oriented, and introspective. They value emotional closeness and intellectual connection, and they look for depth and purpose in relationships. To support them, engage in deep conversations but also respect their need for solitude and introspection. Acknowledge their natural wisdom and intuitive insights while encouraging them to pursue learning and personal development. Shared values and spiritual connectedness will help you build a partnership grounded in mutual understanding and respect for each other's spiritual development.

A PARTNER WITH LIFE PATH NUMBER 8

If your partner has Life Path Number 8, they'll be ambitious, driven, and focused on succeeding in both life and relationships. They assume authoritative roles and place a high value on financial security. To support them best, show your own determination and ambition in pursuing shared goals and dreams. Acknowledge their efforts, hard work, and dedication by providing them with encouragement and practical advice. A spirit of partnership founded on trust, respect, and a shared vision for future goals will help you both flourish.

A PARTNER WITH LIFE PATH NUMBER 9

A companion with a Number 9 Life Path Number is a natural humanitarian, someone who is both transformative and philanthropic. They place a high value on changing the world for the better and look for interactions with others that are meaningful and deep. Acts of compassion and harmony, as well as your own dedication to social justice and helping others, can be used to support them. Encourage harmony and understanding within the relationship by openly appreciating diversity, uniqueness, and enlightenment.

A PARTNER WITH LIFE PATH MASTER NUMBER 11

A partner who has Master Number 11 as their Life Path Number is naturally intuitive, spiritually aware, and highly influential. They have a strong feeling of purpose in life and an acute understanding of how everything is interrelated. To support them, encourage open communication and honor their intuitive insights and influence. Explore a sense of spiritual connection and mutual growth, delving into deeper dimensions of consciousness together. Accept their influence and sensitivity, cultivating a relationship based on compassion, authenticity, and common spiritual principles.

A PARTNER WITH LIFE PATH MASTER NUMBER 22

A companion who has Life Path Master Number 22 is visionary, practical, and capable of significant achievements. They can make dreams come true because they have a unique blend of idealism and practicality. To assist a partner with Master Number 22, offer motivation and useful assistance, acknowledging their capacity to make a lasting impact. Work together toward ambitious projects and goals, all while leveraging each other's strengths. Encourage a strong feeling of purpose and resolve to build a relationship based on common goals and a dedication to changing the world.

A PARTNER WITH LIFE PATH MASTER NUMBER 33

A relationship with a person who has Master Number 33 as their Life Path Number will be incredibly rewarding. This person is a wise, compassionate, spiritual teacher. They are incredibly kind and have a strong feeling of duty to mankind. Provide a safe space for them to express their creative impulses and spiritual insights. Urge them to use their creativity and teaching abilities for serving others, honoring their role as a light of love and compassion. Encourage a partnership grounded in spiritual development, mutual respect, and a shared commitment to making the world a better place.

Your Partner's Numerology

1. How do the qualities associated with your partner's numerological profile resonate with your experiences with them?

....

....

....

....

2. In what ways can understanding your numerological influences deepen your bond and help you communicate?

....

....

....

....

3. After considering your numerological insights, what changes or steps can you take to better connect with your authentic self and build satisfying relationships?

....

....

....

....

FAMILY, COLLEAGUES, AND OTHER RELATIONSHIPS

Most beginners do their first numerology readings for their romantic partners, and this is a great place to start. It's exciting to learn about each other's core traits and gain insight into how you overlap and complement one another. But as you become more adept at performing readings, you can invite more people in your life to learn with you. You might ask family members, trusted colleagues, or friends if they'd be interested in their charts. Then see how your numbers mesh and clash. You can even perform numerology readings for your pets!

Although each type of relationship has its own dynamics, the descriptions in the previous section on romantic partners will give you a good starting point for most of them. A coworker or beloved aunt with Life Path Number 2 will have many of the same traits and needs as a romantic partner and will flourish under the same type of support. Use your intuition to adjust those descriptions as needed, but use them as your foundation when you read for any person (or animal!) in your life.

And just as you advise others that numerology isn't a foolproof fortune-telling system or way to avoid tough choices, keep those things in mind for yourself, too. This tool is like a mirror into your deepest soul: it only reflects back what is already there. Your job is to see and acknowledge that reflection and then take bold, authentic action to honor it.

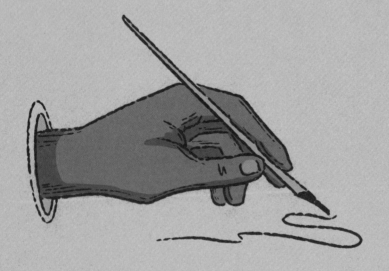

CONCLUSION

Congratulations on finishing your numerology workbook! It's a great way to commit to your personal development and self-discovery. You can keep track of all your numerology findings on a special page that we've included to celebrate your accomplishments. This area is intended to support you as you continue to explore the intriguing field of numerology by recording your discoveries, patterns, and observations. Utilize it to capture your ideas, emotions, and revelations so that you have a visual documentation of your path to increased self-awareness and understanding.

I hope you had fun on this life-changing adventure and that numerology will be a useful resource for you as you continue to investigate and discover the mysteries of your numerological blueprint.

- Life Path Number
- Birth Day Number
- First Impression Number
- Inner Soul (Soul Urge) Number
- Character Number
- Expression Number
- Personal Year Number
- Personal Month Number
- Karmic Lesson Number

- Personal Day Number
- Maturity Number
- Karmic Debt Number
- Birth Path Chart
- Name Chart
- Concords
- Arrows
- In love

Think back on the adventure you've taken with this book and the abundance of knowledge you've acquired about your numerological blueprint and yourself. Each chapter has provided a window into various aspects of your personality, abilities, and possible obstacles, ranging from identifying your Life Path Number to delving into the nuances of your Birth Path Chart and Name Chart.

It's time to put together the pieces of information you've learned and identify the patterns that have emerged. Do you see how your Birth Day Number and Inner Soul Number, as well as your Life Path Number and Expression Number, impact each other in subtle but significant ways? Notice how the general themes and energies of particular times in your life are shaped by your Month and Year Numbers and how your Karmic Expression Number and Maturity Number provide information about how you have changed and grown over time. There's so much to see!

Think about the meaning of your Karmic Debt Number and the ways it might show up in your personal growth, professional life, and relationships. Examine the relationship between Concords and Arrows in your numerology charts to identify places that may benefit from development and transformation as well as harmonic alignments.

Always remember to approach the process of delving further into the details of your numerological profile with an open mind, curiosity, and compassion for yourself. Accept the process of self-discovery as an ongoing and evolving exploration, and give yourself permission to follow your intuition with introspection.

Finally, recognize the useful applications of numerology in various aspects of your life, whether it's understanding your compatibility in love, navigating difficult behavioral patterns, or even gaining insights into your relationships with pets. You can continue to use numerology's insights to build even more self-awareness, fulfillment, and harmony in all aspects of your life by incorporating this practice into your daily routine with mindfulness and intention.

- How has your understanding of numerology progressed throughout this journey, and what insights have resonated with you the most?
- In what ways have you noticed patterns or connections between different aspects of your numerological profile, and how do they reflect your personality, strengths, and areas for growth?
- Reflecting on your numerology charts, what surprises or discoveries have you encountered that have deepened your understanding of yourself and your life path?
- Going forward, how do you plan to apply the insights and applications of numerology to your everyday life? What actions will you take to be true to who you are and reach your full potential?

Resources

························

NUMEROLOGY ONLINE

astrology.com/numerology

Although numerology isn't its main focus, this trusted site does a fabulous job of summarizing the history and basics of numerology.

FOR MORE ON NUMEROLOGY AND TAROT

tabi.org.uk/2020/08/tarot-tutorial-beginners-guide-to-the-use-of-numerology-in-tarot-readings

This post, "A Beginner's Guide to the Use of Numerology in Tarot Readings," offers a helpful primer on the intersection of numerology and tarot.

LEARN MORE ABOUT ARROWS

yourzodiacsign.com/numerology/arrows

The Arrows in Numerology Grids: Digs deeper into both the set of Arrows we explored in this book, and a few more!

ALL ABOUT THE CONCORDS

visiblebynumbers.com/f/the-concords

This entry from numerologist Alison Baughman's fantastic blog provides a helpful overview of the Concords.

Index

. . . .

#

11 (Master Number), 17, 46–
48, 169, 202
in Core Numbers, 63, 71,
80, 88, 97, 107
in Cycle Numbers, 119–20,
127, 135, 147
22 (Master Number), 17, 45,
49–51, 169, 202
in Core Numbers, 64, 71,
80, 88–89, 97–98, 107–8
in Cycle Numbers, 120,
136, 147–48
33 (Master Number), 17, 45,
52–54, 169, 203
in Core Numbers, 64, 80,
89, 98, 108
in Cycle Numbers,
120, 148

A

abundance, 25–26, 39, 63, 80,
169, 207
and Core Numbers, 70, 79,
88, 97, 107
and Cycle Numbers, 119,
127, 153
gold symbolizing, 51
and jade, 29
accountability, 27–29, 33, 96,
106, 146, 157

Activity, Arrow of, 185,
191, 192
adaptability, 30–31, 201
and Core Numbers, 62, 69,
78, 87, 96, 106
and Cycle Numbers, 118,
126, 134, 146
adventure, 30–32, 169, 176,
185, 201, 207
and astrology, 25,
43–44, 53
and Core Numbers, 62, 69,
78, 87, 96, 106
and Cycle Numbers, 117–
18, 126, 134, 146, 153
aging, 138, 145, 147
ambition, 18, 39, 49, 107,
169, 199
and Arrow of
Determination, 184
and astrology, 28, 40–41,
43–44, 50–51
and business
partnerships, 181
and Core Numbers,
63–64, 70–71, 79–80,
88, 95, 97
and Cycle Numbers, 117,
121, 135, 147, 153
and romantic
relationships, 201–2
amethyst, 38
Angelou, Maya, 24

anomalies, 171, 176
apricot (color), 23
aqua, 32
aquamarine, 32
Aquarius, 28, 40–41, 47–48
archetype, 17, 19, 22, 25,
27–28, 31
definition of, 14
Aries, 19, 43–44
Arrows, 14, 163, 184–
93, 208–9
See also specific Arrow charts
artistic expression, 24, 77, 80,
169, 178, 182
and Arrow of Creativity,
185, 191
in Core Numbers, 105
in Cycle Numbers, 117,
125, 133, 145, 153
and romantic
relationships, 200
astrology, 10, 20, 22, 37
See also specific zodiac signs
awakenings, 42, 97, 119, 127

B

Babylon, 11
Bach, Johann Sebastian, 33
Baughman, Alison, 209
beauty, 24, 34, 35, 133
Beyoncé, 27

Birth Chart, 26, 178, 180, 184, 186, 189

birth date, 9, 12–14, 57, 67, 165, 180
    for Arrow chart, 186, 188
    for Cycle Numbers, 15, 115–16, 138–39, 150, 155
    for Life Path Number, 10, 15, 58–60
    to perform readings, 179, 196, 198

Birth Day Number, 14, 66–72, 110, 208

birth name, 12–13, 180, 188, 196, 198
    for Core Numbers, 14, 57, 73–74, 82–83, 91–92, 101
    for Cycle Numbers, 15, 140–43, 151
    for Name Chart, 15, 173–75, 177
    See also chosen name

Birth Path Chart, 14, 164–70, 172, 177

Birth Path Number, 167–70

birthstones, 20
    See also specific birthstones

black, 41

black tourmaline, 41

blue, light, 32

Branson, Sir Richard, 49

brown, 41

Buddhism, 24, 36

Buffet, Jimmy, 24

business, 135, 178–81, 183
    unfinished, 15, 154, 171

C

Cancer, 22–23, 37

Capricorn, 28, 40–41, 50–51

career, 21, 33, 61, 64, 183, 192
    and Birth Day Number, 72
    and Cycle Numbers, 121, 135
    and job loss, 157

Carrey, Jim, 42

Chaldean numerology, 12

Character Number, 14, 91–99, 111

Chariot, 37

Chinese numerology, 11–12

chosen birth day, 13

chosen name, 13, 140, 151, 173
    and Core Numbers, 74, 83, 92, 101

Christianity, 24

citrine, 26

clear quartz, 54

Clinton, Bill, 46

collaboration, 22, 34, 42, 169, 196, 200
    in business partnerships, 178
    and Core Numbers, 77, 86, 95
    and Cycle Numbers, 125, 145, 153, 157

communication, 15, 34, 157, 176, 184, 189

and Core Numbers, 61, 68, 86, 91, 95, 100
and first impressions, 14, 73, 77
in performing readings, 196–98
in relationships, 181, 199–202, 204
skills in, 21, 24–25, 30–32, 105

compassion, 13, 35, 198, 201–3, 208
    Arrow of, 184–85, 190
    in Core Numbers, 69, 77–80, 87–89, 96, 98, 106–8
    in Cycle Numbers, 118, 120, 133–34, 146–48, 157
    and Pisces, 25, 47
    and tarot cards, 34, 40, 43
    value of, 21, 33, 42, 52–54, 62–64

compatibility, 14, 163, 178, 180–81, 198–99, 208

Concords, 14, 163, 178–83, 198, 208–9

confidence, 45, 105, 164, 169, 190, 197
    and Core Numbers, 61, 64, 86, 88, 91, 97
    and Cycle Numbers, 117, 125, 133, 153
    inspiring, 18, 41
    and Leo, 19
    and sun, 20
    and tarot cards, 40

confidentiality, 197, 198

consonants, 14, 75, 83, 91–93, 172

coral (color), 23

Core Numbers, 12–14, 55, 57, 110–11, 113, 160–61
    Master Number as, 15, 17
    in performing readings, 196
    See also specific names of Core Numbers

creativity, 20–26, 32, 35, 49, 52, 64
    and 0, 55
    Arrow of, 184–85, 191–93
    and astrology, 19, 25, 28, 40, 47–48, 53
    in Birth Path, 169
    in business partnerships, 179
    in Concord grouping, 182
    and Core Numbers, 61, 86, 89, 95, 98
    and Cycle Numbers, 114, 117, 125, 133, 145, 153
    and development, 30
    in expression, 68, 100, 105, 107–8
    and first impressions, 73, 77, 80
    inspiration for, 38
    and Mars, 45
    and repeat numbers, 176
    in romantic partners, 200, 203

crimson, 44–45

crystals, 9, 26, 38, 48

curiosity, 30, 32, 106, 146, 208

in astrology, 25, 31, 44
in romantic relationships, 201
and tarot, 50

cycles, 30–31, 42, 43, 55, 122
    natural, 24, 27

Cycle Numbers, 10, 12, 113, 154, 158–60
    See also specific names of Cycle Numbers

D

Dalai Lama, 49

da Vinci, Leonardo, 24

de la Renta, Oscar, 18

dependability, 22, 27, 33–34, 171, 200
    and Core Numbers, 62, 69, 78, 86, 106

destiny, 9, 14–15, 100, 113, 163, 172
    and Cycle Numbers, 119, 127, 150

determination, 18, 20, 41, 45, 49, 169
    Arrow of, 184, 189
    in astrology, 19, 28, 44
    and Birth Day Number, 68, 70
    in Concords, 178, 180
    in Core Numbers, 63, 77, 79, 86, 95, 105
    in Cycle Numbers, 133, 150
    embracing, 27
    in performing readings, 197

in romantic partners, 199–201
in tarot cards, 37

Diana, Princess, 36

Dickinson, Emily, 33

diligence, 27, 29, 153, 169, 200
    in Core Numbers, 69, 78, 86, 95, 105

diplomacy, 21, 34, 153, 169, 200
    in Core Numbers, 61, 66, 68, 77, 86, 95, 105
    in Cycle Numbers, 117, 125, 133, 145, 153

discipline, 28–29, 37, 39–41, 185
    in Core Numbers, 79, 88, 107
    in Cycle Numbers, 118, 125, 134, 136, 157

Disney, Walt, 18

diversity, 12, 34, 36, 79
    of experiences, 24, 30–31, 126, 185, 202

drive, 39, 44–45, 58, 169, 185, 201
    in Arrow charts, 189, 190
    in Concord analysis, 181

E

Earhart, Amelia, 39

Earnhardt, Dale, 49

Eastwood, Clint, 27

Edison, Thomas, 52

Einstein, Albert, 52

empathy, 21, 33–34, 42, 46, 52, 169
in Arrow charts, 185, 190
in astrology, 37, 47, 53
and Character Number, 95–96
and Core Numbers, 68, 71, 77, 80, 86, 88–89
and Cycle Numbers, 120, 133, 135, 147–48, 153
and Expression Number, 105, 107
and Life Path Number, 62–64
in performing readings, 195, 197
in romantic relationships, 199–201
Emperor (tarot card), 27–28
empowerment, 11, 20, 66, 100, 113, 164
and karmic debt, 154, 171
in Name Chart, 172
of others, 80, 89
in performing readings, 195–98
Empress (tarot card), 25
enlightenment, 38, 42, 44, 47, 50, 52
in Core Numbers, 62–63, 70, 79–80, 88, 97, 106–7
in Cycle Numbers, 119, 127, 134–35
in Name Chart, 172
in performing readings, 195
with romantic partners, 202

spiritual, 36, 43, 46, 53–54, 169
escapism, 42, 47
ethics, 13, 47, 157
work, 28, 62, 69, 106
Expression Number, 14, 100–9, 111, 161, 208

F

family values, 33, 35, 96, 106, 169, 201
in astrology, 22–23
and Concord analysis, 179
and Cycle Numbers, 118, 126, 134, 146, 153
finances, 97, 107, 157, 169, 201
and Cycle Numbers, 119, 127, 135, 147, 153
First Impression Number, 14, 73–81, 110
Fool (tarot card), 50
Ford, Henry, 39
freedom, 25, 30–31, 169, 200
and Core Numbers, 62, 69, 78, 87, 96, 106
and Cycle Numbers, 118, 126, 134, 146, 153
friends, 68–69, 86, 114, 145
connections with, 77, 133, 178
performing readings for, 195–96, 198, 205
Frustration, Arrow of, 184

G

garnet, 20

Gates, Bill, 27
Gemini, 31
gemstones, 10
See also specific gemstones
gold, 51
green, 25, 29

H

harmony, 11, 32, 42, 82, 169, 208
in astrology, 22–23, 34, 43–44, 47, 53
and Birth Day Number, 66, 68–70
and Concords, 14, 180
and Core Numbers, 77, 79, 86, 88, 95–97, 105–7
creating, 21–22, 33, 35
and Cycle Numbers, 117–18, 125–26, 129, 133–34, 145
and karma, 150, 153, 155
and Life Path Number, 58, 61
in natural world, 46
in relationships, 178–81, 199–202
with universe, 29, 43, 48, 51, 54
Hawking, Stephen, 39
healing, 33, 35, 52–54, 182
and karmic debt, 156–57, 171, 176
promoting, 23, 68, 86, 120, 148
health, 68, 86, 157
Hepburn, Audrey, 33

Hermit (tarot card), 43

Hierophant (tarot card), 31

High Priestess (tarot card), 22

Hinduism, 36

humanitarianism, 42, 44–45,
    169, 185, 190, 202
  in astrology, 28, 47–48
  in Core Numbers, 63, 70,
    79, 97–98, 107
  in Cycle Numbers, 147
  and karma, 153, 157

I

independence, 18, 28, 43–44,
    169, 185, 199–201
  in Core Numbers, 66, 68,
    77, 86, 95, 105
  in Cycle Numbers, 117,
    122, 125, 133, 145, 153

indigo, 35

individuality, 18, 20, 48, 200

Inner Soul Number, 14, 82–
    90, 111, 208

inspiration, 25, 38, 44, 153,
    182, 190
  in Core Numbers, 69–71,
    73, 80, 86, 88, 106–7
  in Cycle Numbers,
    117, 120, 125, 129,
    133, 135–36
  in Life Path Number,
    61, 63–64
  and Master Numbers, 15,
    17, 46, 176
  and Maturity Number,
    138, 145–48

source of, 18, 24,
    42, 49, 182
integrity, 27, 40, 47, 157

Intellect, Arrow of, 184, 189

intellectuality, 12, 31–32, 36,
    38, 53, 58
  in Arrow charts, 184, 189
  in Core Numbers, 62, 70,
    79, 87, 96, 106
  in Cycle Numbers,
    106, 134
  in relationships, 182, 201

interconnectedness, 22, 33,
    42, 63, 179

introspection, 38, 43, 62, 157,
    169, 208
  in astrology, 37, 50–51
  and Core Numbers, 70,
    79, 96, 106
  and Cycle Numbers,
    114, 118, 126, 134,
    146, 153–54
  and Karmic Debt Numbers,
    154, 157
  promoting, 35–36, 48, 198
  in romantic
    relationships, 201

intuition, 21, 35–36, 38, 185,
    201–2, 208
  in astrology, 22–23, 25, 37
  and Character
    Number, 95–97
  and Core Numbers, 68, 71,
    77, 80, 86, 88
  and Cycle Numbers, 119–
    20, 126–27, 134–35, 147

and Expression
    Number, 105–7
  and Life Path
    Number, 58, 63
  and Master Numbers,
    15, 46–48, 50–51, 53,
    169, 176
  in performing readings,
    196–97, 205
  and tarot cards, 19, 22, 43

Islam, 36

J

jade, 29

Jobs, Steve, 18

Jolie, Angelina, 30

Jordan, Michael, 46

Judaism, 11, 36

Jupiter, 26, 54

Justice (tarot card), 47

K

Kabbalah, 11

karma, 41, 155–57, 176, 186
  imbalance of, 15, 150, 154

Karmic Debt Number, 15,
    17, 154–57, 159–60,
    189, 208

Karmic Expression
    Number, 208

Karmic Lesson Number, 15,
    150–53, 159

Karmic Numbers, 10, 171, 176

Kennedy, John F., 36

kindness, 54, 185, 190, 196,
200–1, 203
in Core Numbers, 61, 68,
86, 97, 107
in Cycle Numbers, 120,
134, 147
King, Stephen, 52
King Jr., Martin Luther, 18
Knowles, Beyoncé
Giselle, 140–44

L

labradorite, 48
lapis lazuli, 51
leadership, 18–20, 28,
39, 52, 169
and Arrows, 184, 190
in Core Numbers, 66, 68,
86, 88, 95, 97–98
and Cycle Numbers, 120,
145, 147, 153
and Expression Number,
100, 105, 107–8
and first impressions,
73, 77, 79
and Life Path Number,
61, 63–64
in relationships, 181, 200
in tarot cards, 19, 31, 43
Lee, Bruce, 36
Lennon, John, 52
Leo, 19
Libra, 34
Life Path Number, 10, 58–65,
110, 161, 164, 182
definition of, 15

and Expression
Number, 208
and Karmic Debt
Number, 155
of partners, 199–203
Lincoln, Abraham, 30
Lovers (tarot card), 33–34

M

Madonna, 21
Magician (tarot card), 19
Major Arcana, 22, 28, 31, 33,
37, 40, 43
definition of, 19
Empress and Emperor
in, 25, 27
and Master
Numbers, 47, 50
Malcolm X, 30
Mandela, Nelson, 39
manifestation, 39, 48, 51–
52, 55, 170
and Core Numbers, 72,
81, 90, 99
and Cycle Numbers, 120–
21, 136, 152, 156
and Master Numbers,
171, 176
and tarot cards, 19, 25
Marley, Bob, 42
maroon, 44–45
married name, 13, 74, 83, 92,
101, 140
for Karmic Lesson
Number, 151
for Name Chart, 173

Mars, 44–45
Master Numbers, 15, 17, 45,
171, 176–78
*See also specific Master
Numbers (11, 22, and 33)*
Maturity Number, 15, 138–49,
159, 208
McCartney, Paul, 49
McConaughey, Matthew, 49
mediation, 21, 61, 68, 77,
86, 95, 145
meditation, 31, 43, 118,
126, 134
with crystals, 26, 38, 54
with gemstones, 20, 23,
29, 32, 35
Mercury, 32
Middleton, Kate, 24
mindfulness, 20, 40, 50, 208
missing letters, 172
missing numbers, 171, 176–77
Monroe, Marilyn, 30
moon, 22–23
moonstone, 23
Mother Teresa, 42
Musk, Elon, 36

N

name, 13, 100, 150, 186, 196
Name Chart, 15, 163, 172–
79, 180, 187, 189
See also birth name;
chosen name
natural world, 11, 25, 33,
39, 46, 49

natural world, *continued*
  cycles in, 24, 27, 30, 122
Neptune, 38
numerology, history of, 11–12

O

Obama, Barack, 46
opposites, 22, 33, 46, 183
optimism, 24–26, 53
  in Core Numbers, 61, 68,
    77, 86, 95, 105
  in Cycle Numbers, 117,
    125, 133, 145
orange, 23

P

Paltrow, Gwyneth, 21
partnerships, 21, 34, 117,
    122, 125
  business, 178–81
  romantic, 179–80, 199–205
past lives, 15, 150, 154, 156
patterns, 10, 14–15, 36, 49,
    170–71, 207–8
  in Arrow charts,
    184, 186–87
  in Core Numbers,
    65, 82, 91
  and Cycle Numbers, 113,
    150, 152, 154
  in Name Chart,
    176–77, 184
  in nature, 39
peach (color), 23
Perry, Katy, 24

Personal Day Number, 14–15,
    129–37, 158
personality, 14, 20, 171, 184,
    192, 207–8
  and Chaldean
    numerology, 12
  and Character Number, 91
  and charts, 163–64, 167,
    172, 175–77
  and Concords, 180
  and Core Numbers, 57, 66,
    72–73, 82, 100, 170
  and Cycle Numbers, 146
  insights into, 10, 164
  and performing
    readings, 196
  in romantic relationships,
    198, 200
Personal Month Number, 15,
    122–28, 158, 208
Personal Year Number, 15,
    114–21, 158, 161, 208
  and Personal Day Number,
    129, 131–32
  and Personal Month
    Number, 124
pets, 205, 208
philanthropy, 42, 202
  and Core Numbers, 70, 79,
    88, 97, 107
Pisces, 25, 37, 47–48, 53
Pluto, 51
practicality, 27–29, 31, 49–51,
    184, 200, 202
  and Birth Day
    Number, 69, 71

  in Core Numbers, 78, 80,
    86, 88, 95, 105
  in Cycle Numbers, 145, 147
  and Life Path
    Number, 62, 64
Presley, Elvis, 42
privacy, 13, 197, 198
purple, 38
Pythagoras, 11, 12

R

readings, 13, 195–205
Reagan, Ronald, 21
red, 20, 44–45
red jasper, 44
Reeve, Christopher, 33
relationships, 21–23, 33–
    34, 41, 178–83,
    199–205, 208
  and Arrows, 192
  and Birth Path
    Number, 169–70
  and Character
    Number, 95, 99
  and Core Numbers, 61, 66,
    68–72, 78, 81, 87, 90
  and Cycle Numbers, 117–
    18, 121, 125–26, 129,
    133–34, 145–46
  and Expression Number,
    105–6, 109
  harmonious, 14, 35, 42
  and karma, 153, 157
  of numbers, 17, 163
repeat letters, 172

repeat numbers, 150, 171, 176–77, 180, 184–85, 188

resilience, 24, 30, 39–41, 44, 68, 160
  and Arrows, 184, 189
  and Birth Path Chart, 164
  and Cycle Numbers, 117, 125, 146
  in tarot cards, 37

responsibility, 13, 27, 33, 39, 41–42, 169
  and Arrows, 190
  in astrology, 25, 40
  and Core Numbers, 62, 64, 69, 78, 87–88, 96, 106
  and Cycle Numbers, 118, 120, 126, 148, 153, 157
  and romantic relationships, 200–1
  and tarot cards, 28, 47

Roosevelt, Eleanor, 33

rose quartz, 35

Rowling, J. K., 24

S

safe space, 197, 203

Sagittarius, 25, 53

Saturn, 29, 40–41

Scorpio, 43–44, 50–51

self-awareness, 18, 27, 160, 164, 177, 207–8
  and Core Numbers, 58, 66, 68, 82
  and Cycle Numbers, 138, 154, 156
  and performing readings, 196, 199
  and tarot cards, 53

self-control, 27, 29, 40–41, 50, 145, 157

self-discovery, 10–11, 18, 32, 36, 160, 207–8
  and Arrows, 185
  and astrology, 44
  and Cycle Numbers, 113, 117, 125, 133, 135
  in performing readings, 196–98
  in relationships, 199
  and tarot cards, 37, 43

self-expression, 24, 32, 86, 95, 105, 169
  and Arrows, 184, 191
  and Cycle Numbers, 117, 125, 133, 145, 153
  and Name Chart, 176
  in romantic relationships, 200

selflessness, 42, 52, 54, 70, 88, 169
  and Cycle Numbers, 119–20, 127, 147, 157

sensitivity, 21–23, 25, 46–47, 53, 185, 202
  and Core Numbers, 71, 80, 88, 97, 105, 107
  and Cycle Numbers, 119, 127, 135, 145
  in performing readings, 195

Shakespeare, William, 36

silver, 48

sociability, 24, 31, 77, 86, 95, 105, 200

social justice, 28, 63, 70, 97, 107, 202

Soul Urge Number, 14, 82, 161
  See also Inner Soul Number

Spielberg, Steven, 30

spirituality, 9–10, 36, 46, 153, 168–69, 182
  development in, 171, 176–77, 184
  in romantic relationships, 201

spontaneity, 24, 96, 106, 169, 181, 185
  and Cycle Numbers, 117–18, 125–26, 133–34, 153
  in romantic relationships, 200–1
  in tarot cards, 50

stability, 27–29, 39, 41, 44, 169, 171
  in astrology, 22–23, 34
  and Core Numbers, 62, 69, 78, 86–87, 95–96, 105–6
  and Cycle Numbers, 118, 125, 145, 153
  and romantic relationships, 200

Stewart, Martha, 39

Streep, Meryl, 52

Strength (tarot card), 40

sun, 20

Swift, Taylor Alison, 74–76

T

tarot, 10, 209

  See also specific tarot cards

Taurus, 22–23, 34

teachings, 10–11, 30–31, 39, 46, 52–53, 169

  and Core Numbers, 64, 80, 82, 89, 98, 108

  and Cycle Numbers, 120, 148, 150, 161

  and romantic relationships, 203

Tesla, Nikola, 36

Thatcher, Margaret, 27

transformation, 9, 30, 42, 49, 153, 208

  and astrology, 44, 47, 50–51

  and charts, 163, 169, 176

  and Core Numbers, 63, 70–71, 79–80, 89, 97, 107–8

  and Cycle Numbers, 15, 113, 119, 126–27, 135, 148

  and romantic relationships, 202

  in tarot cards, 31, 43, 52

trust, 19, 22, 33, 38, 50, 55

  and Core Numbers, 62, 69, 78, 87, 95, 106

  and Cycle Numbers, 114, 119, 127, 135, 146

  and performing readings, 195–96, 205

and romantic relationships, 200–2

turquoise, 32

U

unity, 33, 42, 46, 53, 68, 70

  fostering, 61, 169

Uranus, 40, 48

V

Venus, 35

versatility, 30–31, 153, 169, 201

  and Core Numbers, 62, 69, 78, 96, 106

violet, 35, 38

Virgo, 31

vowels, 14, 74–75, 82–84, 92–93, 172

W

Walters, Barbara, 24

Washington, George, 18

Watson, Emma, 21

white, 54

wholeness, 42, 53, 55

Wicca, 24

William, Prince, 46

Williams, Serena Jameka, 92–94

willpower, 19, 95, 184

Winfrey, Oprah, 27

wisdom, 11, 46, 52–54, 62–63, 160, 169

  and Core Numbers, 64, 68, 71, 80, 89, 96–98, 106

  inner, 35, 37–38, 47, 118–19, 126–27, 134

  intuitive, 48, 51, 97

  and maturity, 15, 146, 148

  and performing readings, 196–97

  practical, 120, 136

  and relationships, 178, 199, 201, 203

  in tarot cards, 22, 31, 40, 43

Woods, Tiger, 18

World (tarot card), 52–53

Y

Y as vowel, 92–93

yellow, 26

yin and yang, 21

Z

zero, 55

zodiac. *See* astrology

Acknowledgments

....

I am deeply grateful to my husband, my mom, my three children, and my extended family for their unwavering love, encouragement, and support throughout the journey of writing this book. Your belief in me and your willingness to stand by my side as I pursued my dreams have been the greatest blessings in my life. Thank you for your patience, understanding, and constant encouragement, even during the most challenging times.

I also express my heartfelt appreciation to my family and friends who have cheered me on every step of the way. Your words of encouragement, acts of kindness, and unwavering support have fueled my passion and inspired me to keep pushing forward, even when faced with obstacles.

To my fans, I am endlessly grateful for your loyalty and support over the years. Your enthusiasm for my work and your continued patronage of my businesses have been a constant source of motivation and inspiration.

Thank you all for being a part of this incredible journey. Your love, support, and belief in me have made all the difference, and I am forever grateful for each one of you.

About the Author

Kelli Miller is a psychic and medium with over 10 years of experience. Kelli is dedicated to guiding others as a spiritual development teacher and mentor. As a transformational speaker, Kelli inspires audiences with her unique insights and wisdom, helping them maximize their full spiritual and personal potential. Kelli is the CEO of Awakenings, which is a huge selection of metaphysical supplies designed to support your spiritual journey, and is based in Omaha, Nebraska.

About the Illustrator

Coni Curi is a self-taught illustrator from Buenos Aires, Argentina. Her style is known as "neo-nostalgia," as she combines vintage style with nowadays topics. Besides being an illustrator, she is a tarot reader and has illustrated several tarot decks. Visit Coni on Instagram @conicuri and at conicuri.com.

INSIGHT. WISDOM. INTUITION.

Decode the secrets of the universe with this indispensable guide to harnessing the hidden truths of your life path.

Your essential workbook to unlock the wisdom of the stars and understand astrology and your birth chart.

zeitgeistpublishing.com

Don't miss this bestselling essential guide to reading tarot cards with confidence and ease.

No deck? No problem! This reader-beloved box set includes *Guided Tarot* and a vibrant Rider Waite Smith tarot deck.

Adapted from *Guided Tarot*, this is a must-have for teens ready to embrace the wisdom of their inner voice through tarot cards.

Hi there,

We hope you enjoyed *Guided Numerology Workbook*. If you have any questions or concerns about your book, or have received a damaged copy, please contact customerservice@penguinrandomhouse.com. We're here and happy to help.

Also, please consider writing a review on your favorite retailer's website to let others know what you thought of the book!

Sincerely,

The Zeitgeist Team